CARE TALK

Skilled Communication In Ministry

Shannon Plate

For churches who understand

not only their potential

but their responsibilities.

Table of Contents

1 – Nothing They Can't Do

A church is an amazing organism. Gathering people, whether 20 or 20,000, with a similar vision and shared energy can lead to astounding results – God praised, people fed, needs met, prayer multiplied, healing had, and care given. When a church acts with pure motivation and wise guidance, there is little it can't accomplish. Faith, prayer, and action encourage each other and become exponentially more powerful. When the people of a church rise to a challenge, there is almost nothing they can't do.

By definition, a church is also a place to which the hurting, both from outside and inside the flock, will flock. Belonging to a church carries with it the knowledge of the support a church can provide. For people not part of a church to take a chance on finding help there in time of crisis, the church is a way to welcome the stranger and introduce them to their first taste of what a relationship with Christ can be like.

The problem with a church is, unfortunately, one of the same things that make it amazing. It's run by people. People, even with fabulous intentions and hearts focused on God, are at best, imperfect. Even giving us all the greatest benefit of the doubt, some things in a church go wrong because we are all still simply sinners – working the process, yes – but, at the end of the day, sinners.

Given perfection, in either word or deed, is out of the question by virtue of our humanness, a church is then given the difficult responsibility of doing what it does at the highest level possible considering what it has to work with – those darn people. Churches have found incredibly creative ways to do that, and little time passes when one doesn't hear of a church somewhere in the world that's come up with a new way to serve each other or the community. I recently came upon a full listing of all the ministries my church runs just out of our building, and I'm embarrassed to say there were a few I didn't even know about, including one that replaces bicycles for people who rely on them to get to work. How cool is that? Churches everywhere provide care ministries that are incredibly creative in using humans, in all our imperfect states, to meet the needs of others.

The thing all Care ministries have in common is the core concept – to help people. There is usually personal contact somewhere along the line, whether from a pastor or other staff to a volunteer, or someone coming for help. In looking for a word to describe the person being served, every church may have their own industry standard term. For our purposes and for the rest of this book, I am going to use "guest," which is how my church describes the people being served in any ministry, whether they are members or someone from the community. They have become, for whatever the need, a guest in God's house, and we are the earthly hosts.

In whatever form, there is ministry taking place for our guest - from a person helping load food from the food pantry into the trunk of a car, to a volunteer teaching a course on budgeting, to a pastor praying over suffering. Help can come in many different forms, but it is usually given through the conduit of a personal interaction.

It is here the church can do better. Tons better. If we are going to offer help, if we sit a staff member or volunteer across from a hurting person, it is our responsibility to make certain the person giving care has been trained how to listen and speak in that situation. A good heart isn't nearly enough. It's a great start, but without instruction in how to make someone feel cared about and understood, we are leaving our Care personnel woefully undereducated and putting a hurting person in danger of leaving the interaction in worse shape than when they arrived.

I am a therapist in private practice. It breaks my heart when someone pays for a session with me to discuss how they were somehow hurt by their church. It could have been feeling disregarded by a pastor in an exchange or leaving a meeting with a volunteer feeling judged or maligned. Even more difficult is the fact that whatever was done may have been with the best of intentions, but without the training necessary to integrate practical or emotional help with an equally caring and trained presence. It is just as much the skill of care as the meeting a physical need that creates comfort at a difficult time.

Though we can't fix all the problems in a church, we can fix this one. Even better news is that it's easily learned, not difficult to do, and it will give you skills you can use to better every relationship of your life.

Welcome to Care Talk.

To begin, not every conversation is the same.

Think of conversations you've had recently, in or out of the church that went well. You walked away feeling good, feeling heard. There may have been agreement, but it would be the cherry on top. The bone-deep satisfaction would be the way the encounter progressed. You were able to say what you wanted to say, and the person with whom you were speaking listened and responded in a way that convinced you they were doing their best to understand you. That is the win for both of you.

Next, think of conversations that happened without much conscious thought. They are neutral, in the sense that they simply don't have the capacity to be life-changing. The words you exchange with the person who checks out your groceries at the store or fixes your glasses can go badly with rudeness on either side, but it is usually not a relationship garnering enough time to warrant more than common courtesy. A person who asks a quick question in the church hallway can be put off by a dismissive tone or look, but it usually has less influence than a full-fledged conversation. It doesn't make it right, but it is probably not worth a session in my office.

Now, think of a conversation that went terribly wrong. Some talks start well and go south quickly or puddle along for a time before ending in a sigh (or something louder), neither party knowing what went badly, but one or both feeling defeated and hopeless at the end. This can happen between staff members talking to each other or between a volunteer working with a food pantry guest or someone coming to the church for help.

Again, this has less to do with finding agreement than it does both parties feeling heard and understood. We are not always going to agree

Ok, brace yourself. Think of a conversation you had recently that went poorly, and you are pretty certain it was your fault. Whoever you were talking to walked away dejected and possibly hurt. You didn't listen well, didn't respond with care, and at the end, you didn't feel good about what happened. The problem was you didn't really know how to do it differently.

This is about to change. The skills you develop from this book will sharply increase your odds of more successful conversations and help you provide care in a way that shows compassion and understanding. There are clear and discernable steps you can take. You can learn and use these skills in the same day. You can practice and get better. You will never ask another "why" question and you will never again say to someone, "I know just how you feel."

If anyone has ever said, "You're not listening to me," you are reading the right book.

This is worth your effort. It will take work and it will take risk. You might make mistakes in the beginning to get better in the end. It will take breaking old patterns and putting new and better ones in place, just like any other improvement you want to make in your life.

Put your boots on and pay attention. There will be a test.

2 – Communicating Care

How many conversations happen in the church in a day? From the first "Good morning," between those early-bird staff members in the office to the last incoming phone call, every interaction makes an impression, be it good or otherwise. You have the opportunity to create connection...or not. You can listen in a way that makes the person speaking feel cared for and treasured. There are definitive ways to do it, and definitive ways to blow it.

Any conversation is about taking turns. There are hardly any interactions that work as a monologue. The key is knowing when and how to add your bit. When to listen and when to talk can be an art form, but, happily for us all, much easier to learn than watercolor.

Consider these two interactions between staff on a Monday morning.

Diane – You'll never guess what happened on Saturday! I called into a radio show and got third row seats to see Lauren Daigle!
Sandy – No way! Wow, the same thing happened to me a couple of years ago. I called in on my way to work and won tickets to go to a ball game on the same day, so I called and told the boss, and he let me go!
Diane – Oh. Yeah, that sounds great.
Sandy – It was! I pulled my son out of school to go with me, and he still calls it the best surprise ever.

Thus ends the conversation. Diane's good news was simply a vehicle for Sandy to tell a similar (and possibly better) story about herself. Perhaps without being aware, she "hogged" the attention of that encounter, and Diane will walk away feeling unheard and, very possibly, annoyed.

A better version of that conversation would be this:

Diane – You'll never guess what happened on Saturday! I called into a radio show and won third row seats to Lauren Daigle!

Sandy – No way! You must be so excited!

Diane – I'm totally excited. She's been my favorite forever. I can't wait. The show is in a couple of weeks, so I'm just going to count down the days.

Sandy – How cool that you got tickets for your favorite. You must feel really lucky!

Diane – I do. The timing had to be just perfect, and I won!

Sandy – Well, congratulations!

Diane – Thanks!

Sandy – You know, the same thing happened to me a couple of years ago. I called in on my way to work and won tickets to go to a ball game on the same day, so I called and told my boss, and he let me go! I pulled my son out of school to go with me, and he still calls it the best surprise ever.

Diane – Really? Wow, you are lucky, too. That must have been so much fun.

Sandy – It was. I love it when unexpected things like that happen. It feels like a total blessing.

Yay! In the second interaction, Sandy took time to take notice of Diane's experience and accompanying feelings. By relating them back, Diane knew Sandy was not just listening in order to respond; she was listening to understand. In less than 25 seconds, it worked — Diane felt understood, Sandy created connection, and at the end, Sandy telling her similar story didn't hijack the conversation. Whether or not to share a similar event is something we will go onto later, but for now, let's say Sandy did well. You go, Sandy.

This is not simply intuitive. Some of it is, in fact, counter-cultural. Left to our own devices, communication can happen without any input at all from another person. We decide for them what they think, feel, and of course, what they should do.

We look at someone's situation, judge their behavior, and decide what we believe would have been a better option. We see someone come to the food pantry in a nice car, and grumble that clearly, they clearly don't need the church's food. In a pastoral care setting, we hear one version of an emotional story and take immediate sides.

We take the available facts, add our opinions, values, and judgment, and call it the truth. We look, we assess, and we decide — sometimes without having (or wanting) any knowledge from the person on whom we are bestowing our great wisdom. We all do this — not just the people that haven't read this book. It's part of our executive functioning, and, like everything else, can be used for good or harm. It does, however, lack prudence and can cause injury in the church or in your home.

The difference is whether we are reacting or responding. Reacting happens internally and often instantly. We take what we think we already know or what our body tells us to do and go with that. Responding happens when we allow time and information to influence our actions, thoughts, and decisions. It is the opposite of saying, "I go with my instinct."

Responding is allowed by waiting — waiting for someone to finish their sentence, waiting for our thoughts to clear, or waiting until we can form a response based on how we choose to reply rather than how we might retort in the moment. It is thoughtful by design and it gets us into much less trouble than reacting. Responding uses all the information available rather than just what we have handy.

A common "reacting" scenario goes like this: Someone tells us about an issue in their lives, and our reaction is to tell them what we would do or think in their place, because, of course, everyone really wants to be us.

Danny and Jordan are working on cars in the church ministry that fixes them for people who can't afford to cover their auto repair costs. Jordan is staff member and Danny a volunteer.

Danny – I'm thinking about buying a new car. There are some good deals out there right now.
Jordan – Wow, I wouldn't do that. I'd get something a couple of years old and let someone else take the hit. If I were you, I'd be looking for a two or three- year-old Subaru. Keeps its value, and good in snow.

Here's the kicker. Nowhere did Danny ask Jordan's advice, and, in fact, the phrase "If I were you" has no place in this conversation. Bad Jordan.

Jordan would be out of the doghouse had he responded more this way:

Danny – I'm thinking about buying a new car. There are some good deals out there right now.
Jordan – Oh, yeah? You sound a little hesitant.
Danny – Well, I'm not sure what to do. If I buy new, it's more expensive but there shouldn't be repair bills for a while. After fixing all these cars, I'm a little scared to buy used. The interest rate on the loan is lower, too, on a new car. If I buy used, there's more risk, the interest rate is higher, and I might end up spending a bunch on repairs.
Jordan – There are pros and cons for each one.
Danny – Yeah. I keep going back and forth.
Jordan – What would be worse? Paying more for a longer time but having some peace of mind about the condition, or taking the chance on something being wrong with a used car, and having to make repairs?

Danny – Really, I want both. I want to buy a used car where I don't have to worry about repairs.

Jordan – OK. Is there any way to do that?

Danny – I wonder if there is a warranty for used cars.

Jordan – When we got our son's car at CarMax, we bought an extended warranty with it, so when he moved away, he could go right to CarMax to get it fixed.

Danny – Wow. I never thought of that. I wonder if other places offer that, too.

Jordan – I'm not sure.

Danny – I bet I can find out. I'll go online and see if other dealerships have them, or if I can buy one for a car I buy on my own. That would be perfect.

Jordan – It's just like insurance. If you never use it, it seems like wasted money, but you seem to be saying it buys you peace of mind.

Danny – You bet. It would totally be worth it. Thanks a lot! I wouldn't have known about this without you telling me.

Jordan – No problem. I hope you find what you want. I have some Consumer Reports magazines on used cars, if you are interested.

Danny – That would be great. Can I get them when I volunteer next week?

Jordan – Sure. I'll bring them then.

Danny – Coffee and donuts are on me!

Nice job, Jordan. Without active listening and basic empathy, all Jordan has is his own opinion and off-the-cuff advice. Throw in a little skill and Danny has a much better idea what he really wants, is willing to work to get it, and feels "talked to" instead of "talked at." Jordan, lucky Jordan, gets donuts.

In a pastoral care setting, it could look like this. A woman losing her apartment has come to the church for help.

Care Pastor – It looks from your paperwork that you will have to leave your apartment in two weeks. Do you have anywhere else you can live?

Donna – Not really. The only person in the area is my mom, and we don't get along well.

Care Pastor – I bet it would work for a little while. She's your mom, after all.

Donna - No, it's hard being with her. My kids don't like it, either.

Care Pastor – It looks like your only choice for now. I had to move back home with my family when I lost my job, and it was hard, but definitely the right move. I think you should really consider it.

I didn't even give that Care Pastor a name. He was that bad. He had nowhere near enough information to even suggest Donna live with her mom and forcing the issue because it worked for him is simply not comparing apples to apples. Let's give him a name and shape him up.

Tony – From your paperwork, it looks like you will have to leave your apartment in two weeks.

Donna – I know. I don't know what to do, though.

Tony – Do you have other options on where to live? Is there anyone you can stay with for a while?

Donna – Not really. The only person in the area is my mom, and we don't get along well.

Tony – It's not a great relationship.

Donna – No, it's not. She drinks a lot, and it's very scary for my kids. They don't even like going there for holidays. Last Easter, she was drinking and ended up screaming at my daughter because she didn't like her Easter dress. She was throwing stuff around and a plate got broken. The kids were terrified.

Tony – You don't feel she's a safe person for you and the kids.

Donna – She really isn't. I can't live with her. I can't put my kids through that.

Tony – There might be other options out there. There are several transitional housing programs in the area. I can print out materials from a couple of websites, if you like.

Donna – That would be great. It wouldn't be ideal, but it would be a lot better than living with her. It's bad enough I have to leave my apartment but going there would be a disaster.

For someone from the church to practically insist Donna live with her mother is inappropriate on so many levels, I hardly know where to start. Two poor scenarios are distinctly possible. One, Donna may follow this terrible advice, and end up in a dangerous situation with her children. Two, Donna will ignore the advice, and leave the meeting feeling angry and frustrated that the Care Pastor pushed an agenda neither investigated nor in her best interests. He still doesn't deserve a name.

The responsibility of the church to treat with respect and care the people God sends into its midst is a heavy one. Great good can be done, but the other side of the coin is to put someone already hurting in worse shape than when they arrived. It's important to note that as a staff person or volunteer, it is easy to take the lead and fully direct any conversation with someone coming to you for help. Not only is it inappropriate from a listening standard, it doesn't leave room for the story or feelings of the other person. It is easy for that person to walk away not just feeling unheard, but also dismissed. Let's not do that.

The same principles are true in terms of how staff communicates. Where should employees treat each other with more consideration than the church? It should be the place where respect and care run rampant; where one can expect fabulous treatment whenever they walk in the door whether coming to work, to service, or receive help.

Jesus was good to nearly everyone, and if He wasn't, there was a very good reason. As we read in Scripture, an occasional holy rebuke wasn't out of the question.

All throughout his Ministry, Jesus knew how to treat people. He spent time and energy communicating well with his followers, yes, but He also cared for and taught his disciples; not just modeling what to do with others but lavishing them with the love He also showed to the public. The washing of their feet in John 13 is a practical and tender reckoning of how Jesus cared for his disciples.

It can sometimes seem to staff that the church cares for the people who come for teaching or help, but may not show care inside its walls before anyone shows up.

Charity begins at home. To show great love and care to those coming in the front doors but not spend time building into and loving the staff can end with resentment and burnout to those entrusted with the important tasks of making the church run.

The same can be true of how the church cares for its volunteers. Most churches couldn't do nearly the good they do without dedicated volunteers but it's easy to overlook the needs of the very groups necessary to do what the staff cannot.

It's no surprise Jesus is the best at what we will be attempting here. All throughout the New Testament, Jesus took the time to listen to people before He spoke, to allow them time to tell their story without judgment or interruption. He did this while already knowing everything about the person He was facing – their past, their future, and what they would do with the words He would give them. We have no such skills, though we sometimes believe we do. We will discuss discernment and its uses and abuses in a later chapter.

Think of the blind man in Mark 10. When he called out to Jesus from begging at the roadside and got His attention, it was clear he was blind. People don't give money to someone without reason – the motivation to give came as a result of his obvious blindness. When Jesus called for him to come, He didn't automatically heal him. He asked the man what he wanted Him to do and listened to the answer. He allowed the man to state his want and need – He took the time to listen.

We can follow that model with friends, family, co-workers and anyone coming through the doors of our church. We don't get to assume we know what they want or need and part of our gift to them is the opportunity to tell their story as we respectfully listen.

The woman at the well in John 4 was shocked when Jesus spoke to her. Samaritans were considered unclean by the Jews, and to speak to a woman was countercultural as well. The fact that she was at the well in the middle of the day might mean she was a social outcast already and used to being ignored or ridiculed. Jesus crossed all kind of lines to engage with her, and though He knew her history and lifestyle, didn't judge, revile, or marginalize her. Through the woman at the well, many people came to Christ. It seems much less likely had Jesus treated her as society and convention dictated.

In Mark, the rich young ruler had everything but eternal life. He came to Jesus wanting the one thing he still needed, hoping his moral life would pay the price asked. When Jesus told him he would have to sell everything and give it to the poor, He knew what the man's answer would be. Jesus knew he would not give up what he had for the eternal life he wanted. The text reads "Jesus loved him," even while knowing what his answer would be.

Like Christ, we need to start with love – for each other as staff and volunteers and for each person individually that walks through our doors. We must start without the filter of our own prejudice, judgment or thoughts of what someone else should do.

No one is saying this is easy. The truth is, however, that it is more Christlike. Since "easy" is not usually in the same sentence as "Christlike," we should prepare ourselves for the challenge that continues to move us toward sanctification. Though difficult, a motivating bonus is the good we will do others with these efforts. Win-win.

13

3 – Choose Your Communication Culture

It starts with this. Here is a concept that could literally change the communication world inside the church, and out.

If we listened to each other — really listened — and responded to what we hear, as opposed to what we <u>think</u> about what we hear, all our relationships would be different.

Please, take a moment and consider this again. The rest of the book and the rest of your life are based on this concept, so we are going to camp here for a while.

Respond to what you hear, not what you think about what you hear.

Respond without adding your opinion, whether you agree or not, or how abysmally wrong (in your opinion) the other person might be. Respond in a way so the person speaking has no earthly idea how you feel on the subject. Before you say it, this does not mean you agree with what is being said — you are merely taking the time to completely understand it. If needed, there will be an appropriate time later to disagree.

Respond to what is being said by the person speaking — on their terms, and without your input or direction. Respond from their worldview, from their viewpoint, and from their personal perspective.

This is far from automatic and no one is born knowing how to do it. To develop this culture is a result of first choosing it, then learning the skills and abilities necessary to implement it, and finally using them with everyone the church touches – staff, volunteers, and guests.

Here's a common type of conversation before the use of this irreplaceable concept.

Alena – I'm thinking about leaving my leadership position in the women's ministry. I'm pretty burned out and I think I need a break.
Irene – I think it's a bad idea to leave now, right when the ministry is reorganizing. I bet you can hold on another year until it's on its feet. I'm tired, too, but I'm going to stay for the good of the ministry. You can do it!

First, Alena, allow me to apologize for even writing that. How dismissed you must feel! Let's shape Irene up and try again.

Alena – I'm thinking about leaving my leadership position in the women's ministry. I'm pretty burned out and I think I need a break.
Irene – Being in leadership has been exhausting. You're feeling like you need to leave to get a rest.
Alena – Yes. I know the timing isn't perfect with the reorganization going on, but there is the thought, too, that it would be a better time now than later. Someone else can be in place and get the full benefit of learning how to do it the new way from the beginning.
Irene – For someone just starting out in leadership, beginning now can give them the full scale of learning it as it changes, rather than coming in later and having to figure it out.
Alena – That's it. I don't think I'm being silly thinking it would work. Are you staying on?
Irene – I think I will for another year, at least. I'm getting tired, too, but I think I have another year in me.

Respond to what you hear, not what you think about what you hear. This time, Irene responded to what she heard Alena say, not how she felt about what Alena said. She can certainly be thinking it is not a decision she would make. She can disagree with Alena on what to do for herself. What helps in her relationship with Alena is to use skills to make her understood, even if later in the conversation she wants to express her opinion.

15

It's important to note that expressing an opposite or personal opinion at the onset of any conversation can often have the effect of making it extremely short. Were I Alena, it would have ended right after Irene's initial comment in the first example.

Respond to what you hear, not what you think about what you hear. Imagine how this would change how we communicate in conflict. Depending on your personality and the style of the person with whom you are arguing, a conflict can look something like those political pundits on TV. They have no interest in what the other person is saying, and there is no possible way one person will sway the opinion of the other. It's not the point of the encounter. They are both concretely solid in their own view, and the only reason to even speak to the other person on the matter is to try and get them to look bad or incompetent with manipulation, volume, and spin. In short, they have no intention of understanding each other.

This is no way to manage a conflict.

Imagine for a moment working hard to listen and understand the other person in a disagreement, to take the time to make sure they are understood before you speak, and to get the same treatment in return. It doesn't usually work this way in conflict, right? Usually, we just talk faster or louder to try and make ourselves heard, and any connection had when we started is long gone when we're finished.

You wouldn't be getting your money's worth without acronyms, so I'm giving you three.

The first is "RTWYH." It's pronounced, "Rotwhy," like the dog. RTWYH. **R**espond **T**o **W**hat **Y**ou **H**ear, also inferring, Not What You Think About What You Hear, because that would be a crazy long acronym.

RTWYH. Respond to what you hear, not what you think about what you hear. You are hearing and responding without it going through the filter of your own worldview, values, or opinions. You aren't deciding whether you agree or disagree – you are listening to understand, not react. Using this concept, you can talk to anyone, anytime, about anything - and make sure the person speaking feels respected and understood. No matter your views on any subject, for peace in the world we need to be able to listen to someone else's opinion without the top of our heads blowing off. You'd be amazed how differently a conversation can go when you start out knowing your goal does not have to be agreeing, forcing the other person to agree with you, or solving whatever issue on which the talk is centered.

Especially in the church, where people come when the wheels fall off (even if they are not a part of the body), it is extremely important that the interaction when they tell their story be kind, attentive, and chock-full to the brim with RTWYH.

RTWYH. Keep a reminder where you can see it — you are going to use it for the rest of your life. Write it down, use the letters as a screensaver, get a tattoo. This is powerful, and it works. If you are talking to someone for any other reason but to tell them their hair is on fire, RTWYH is the way to begin.

The fabulous thing about communicating this way is you get so much more information than when you were just waiting to get your turn to speak. Truly listening nets you a plethora of thoughts and feelings that would otherwise have gone unsaid and unexplored. Paying this kind of attention also gives you the brain space to be sifting and organizing what you're hearing as its being said. We can only do so many things at once, so if we're not searching our minds for a relating story, we have much more capacity to communicate care.

Acknowledging what we are hearing is from the speaker's perspective also frees us from the need to immediately correct inconsistencies or opinions. That in turn leaves time to gather information from what is being said so it can be brought forth later. Here are some important subjects on which you can focus and jot down (either with paper and pen or in your head) to discuss when appropriate.

- What are the main points being discussed?
- What experiences and behaviors are most vivid to the speaker? To you?
- Are there spiritual aspects of the story to discuss?
- Is there a theme present? Do you sense a positive attitude, feelings of entitlement, or a victim mentality?
- What is most important about the story to the speaker?
- Is there anything bothering you about the story? Are there pieces missing, or parts that don't make sense to you?

To be able to grab and keep this level and amount of information is not inherent. If it's a particularly important or serious conversation and you would like to take notes, ask your speaker if it's all right with them. Explain you want to be able to keep everything straight, and it would be helpful to be able to write it down. If they say, "no," do your best without.

When you are done listening and it's your turn to speak, these are some of thing on which you will be empathizing, and on which you might need more information. You might find even though the story was about your co-worker's trip to the emergency room with her son, the most important part of the story to her might be the talk she and her son had right before they stitched him up. Never assume a story's contextual content is paramount — the best part of a volunteer's vacation may well have been one perfect piece of Key Lime pie with the aunt hadn't seen for years, and not the fancy location where it was eaten. The important part of the story is what is important to the speaker.

This is a short, but exceedingly important chapter. I encourage you to go back and read these few pages again. It will be worth your time to get this concept firmly in place.

4 – Let Me Level With You

It's important to discuss the different types of conversations we have. Clearly, not every encounter is the same. For our purposes, we will talk about Level 1 (L1) and Level 2 (L2) discussions.

L1 conversations are the everyday exchanges of information, the chit-chats we do with many different people, often many times a day. "The paperwork you wanted is finished," "What time do I get the kids?" or "I'm off to Bible Study – see you at 9."

L2 conversations are differentiated from L1 by the depth of emotion someone is feeling, a change to more serious subject matter, or the need for one or both parties to be understood. L2 conversations are more work, but also net more results.

With some people, your conversations will stay at L1 forever. Some relationships are not designed to get to L2, whether from the nature of the relationship or the lack of need to go there.

There are exceptions, however. You will occasionally have an L2 discussion with someone you have never seen before or might not see again. In the church, L2 conversations run rampant. Depending on the culture of the church, staff might be encouraged to share their lives more often than the marketplace, and people call or show up at churches they have never attended in times of crisis, thus making any of those conversations L2 by definition.

The moral of the story? Be ready for L2 conversations at every turn.

Let's talk for a few moments about "banter." Banter is defined as "the playful and friendly exchange of teasing remarks." Clearly L1, right? The problem happens when the banter-er doesn't seem to realize there is no "exchange." All the bantering is one way. At that point, it is a distinct possibility it is no longer fun and no longer lighthearted from the viewpoint of the banter-ee.

It's a good idea to pay attention to when and with whom you banter. A deeper thought process is knowing for what reason you banter — but one insight at a time.

Bantering with someone for whom banter is not pleasurable can squash the possibility of ever getting to a L2 conversation and can actually shorten or even end a L1 discussion. Here are a few signs your banter isn't working.

- There is no "exchange." You are the only one tossing around "humorous" comments, one after another.
- After your really funny comment, there is dead silence from the listener, accompanied by a stony-faced expression or a deep sigh.
- The other person leaves your presence in a huff and there is emotional distance that wasn't there before the banter began.

For you to understand what has happened is important. Was this unusual? If banter is a common part of your relationship with this person, it might be simply bad timing or a bad joke that got this response. If this is the usual response, it may be the listener either doesn't appreciate this art form, or they feel the situation warranted a different response. A conversation about their reaction may help you to see if your future witty behavior needs an adjustment or was inappropriate for this particular situation.

Looking at your reasons for bantering can be illuminating. Some banter is just for fun. The back-and-forth comments, barbed or not, can be a riot between people who are a willing part of the conversation, and who typically know each other well. Other reasons for banter lie deeper. Banter can be used manipulatively to shut down conversations the banter-er doesn't want to have.

A couple comes to the church for counsel, the wife complaining about poor communication in the marriage. She relates this conversation as proof.

Anna – We really need to sit down and talk about money. With Will going to college in the fall, we're going to have to batten down the hatches some.

Donny – No problem. I'll just quit eating.

Anna – I mean it. Let's sit down and look at everything.

Donny – In fact, I'll quit eating now. I'll just wither away, getting smaller and smaller, but saving tons of money in the process to send Will to school.

Anna – Please be serious. We need to make some changes.

Donny – How many more changes do you want me to make? I've already quit eating.

Anna – Ok, I give up. I'll do it myself.

Donny – I'd help, but I'm feeling quite weak from hunger.

At this point, Anna turned her back and walked away. As she explains it to the counselor, Donny will never talk about anything serious, and she is left to do everything difficult herself.

With his banter, it looks like Donny accomplished exactly what he wanted. He doesn't have to look at the budget, and if questioned, he can shrug his shoulders. The fact she is hurt by his dodge isn't his fault — she just "doesn't understand" his sense of humor.

Using banter to an extreme to create distance between you and someone else is effective. If the hurtful jokes keep coming, the relationship will never get to a deeper level, and for someone who doesn't want intimacy but doesn't want to say so, it's a useful coping mechanism. If you see yourself here, I might suggest finding out what is so scary about intimacy or honesty, but hey, I'm a therapist. Always looking for new clients. The fact remains an L1 conversation can still have many of the components of a L2 conversation, including the ability to inflict pain.

Most of the quick chat we do via emailing or texting is L1. Some issues occur when those encounters move to L2, and the technology doesn't support that change. The heart of texting is brevity and convenience, and trying to discern feeling and motivation is a stretch. Texting is not famous for nuance. If I had a buck for every time I had to clarify someone's mood or intent in a text, my back yard would be full of deer.

Emailing can be better, but still not best. The more accomplished a writer you are, the more likely your point will get across, but it's best to have L2 conversations with as much connection as possible. In-person communication allows for most of the possible communication data points to take place — sight, intonation, body language, eye contact — and if that's not possible, video chat or a phone call might be the next option. Even if the first shot at something difficult seems better in an email, where you can think out your words and get everything down, at some point a face-to-face meeting for an L2 conversation is probably optimal.

Some talks may begin as a L1 and move to L2 within the conversation. This talk could have been between staff members when they came back after Christmas.

Dorothy — Hey, Dave. What did Santa bring you this year?

Dave — Santa did drop by with those fancy floor mats I wanted for my car.

Dorothy — I'm glad to see he was on the job. Was it a good holiday for your family?

Dave — Well, it's getting clear my dad is suffering from some dementia. A couple things happened while they were in town making us think things are getting much worse.

(This just became L2, right after talking about Santa. It can happen anytime.)

Dorothy — Oh, I'm so sorry. That must have been hard for you.

Dave — You know, my mom has been saying he was getting worse, but we all thought she was being dramatic. Turns out she was right, and we just weren't listening.

Dorothy — It sounds difficult all the way around.

Dave – It was, but now we are in the process of getting them some help. I don't know if they will stay in the house or move, but something will change.

Dorothy – It must be a relief to be working on a plan.

Dave – It will be better when it's done. Anyway, thanks for asking.

Dorothy – Of course! I'll be praying for you all. I hope the New Year brings some good news.

Moving to an L2 talk in the middle of any conversation is in no way unusual, so having your skills at the ready is imperative. It's like an umbrella — you don't always know when you're going to need one, but when you do, nothing else works as well.

Being well-tuned in to any talk you are having is the first step to determining if it is L1 or L2. You should be able to tell quickly if an encounter is starting out as an L2, but if you're not certain, here are a few questions to help you decide.

- What is the level of intensity? The higher the intensity, the more likely it is an L2 talk. Be aware intensity is sometimes camouflaged as volume. If the conversation is getting louder, it's likely someone doesn't feel listened to, and the only way they can think of to get your attention is to pump up the volume.
- Is the subject matter important to the person speaking? The more important the subject to the person speaking, the more likely you are in L2 land.
- Is the other person showing frustration with how the conversation is going? If so, you may want to bump up the skills and assume you are in an L2 talk.

Let's say you are wrong. Let's say you've given L2 time and attention to a talk that was really just L1. What's the worst that can happen? The person with whom you were speaking feels...extra understood? Not quite a tragedy.

This goes without saying, but I'm saying it anyway. Safety first. There may be some people in your life or in your church with whom it is not safe to be face-to-face for any reason. Use your discretion, by all means, and if you have doubts or concerns, check in with other people who know and understand the situation.

To summarize, a good first step is always to determine if you are starting out as an L1 or L2 talk. It's hard to know how to respond without that information. It will help you choose how to move forward.

There is a major tenet that goes along with this concept. It is "Do No Harm." No one should be in worse shape when they leave your presence because of your treatment of them. You may not be able to agree to their viewpoint or be able to provide what they want, but everyone can leave you feeling understood and respected. We, like Jesus with the Rich Young Ruler in Matthew 10:21, need to love them first.

For people we cannot help in the way they believe they need, what we can be is our best in the time we spend together. Determine whether it is L1 or L2 conversation. Are they asking something from us or the church, or just wanting a good listener? Can we put our opinions aside in order to be both objective and kind? For someone to walk away from an encounter feeling unheard, unloved, and dismissed causes harm. Don't think for a second rudeness or flippancy is neutral. It is not.

Do no harm. It will sometimes be the most you can do, but at the root of things, it is also the least you can do.

5 – What's the Magic Word?

James 4:12 But, you – who are you to judge your neighbor?

Here it comes. The word on which all of this is based, and without which our communication would just be a collection of sentences about ourselves, tossed back and forth like a hot potato.

Empathy. Ah, yes. Empathy is what allows us to take our minds and hearts off ourselves. It's how we can see something from a perspective other than our own. It is "other focused" compassion in action.

Empathy is the capacity for understanding another's feelings. It is not "sympathy" — wherein what affects one affects another. Empathy is understanding someone's feelings, not feeling their feelings with them.

It is imperative to get this difference straight. In the United States, these terms are sometimes used interchangeably or even exactly opposite of how they should be. We are using the more clinical definitions for the purpose of working with other people. It is how those two words will be used for the rest of the book, so please take the time to make the difference real in your thoughts.

In Galatians 6:2, it says "Share each other's burdens, and in this way obey the law of Christ." Empathy is the way to respond without becoming part of the burden. It is the way to love and understand one another without having to experience all the same situations. With empathy, we can understand an amazing event or a horrible one by looking at it completely from the perspective of the person that was there. It is the very basis, in fact, for compassion.

An example might help, substituting a physical circumstance in place of an emotional circumstance.

You are standing at a crosswalk of a busy road. You are waiting for your "Walk" sign to come on when you notice one car clearly doesn't see another car, and if they don't do something about it darn soon, they are going to crash. You start waving your arms and yelling, but they don't see you and one car smashes into another. You pull out your phone and call 911, then, watching traffic, run to the first car. You ask everyone in the car if they are all right and tell them the police and fire department are on their way. They all say they are fine, but they are understandably shaken. You assure them again help is on the way and go to the other car. Here, the driver is bleeding from a wound on his shoulder, and his passenger has a huge bump on her head. You put pressure on his wound to slow the bleeding and notice a cold bottle of water rolling around on the floor she can put on her head until the paramedics get there. Again, you tell them help is on the way and stay with them until help arrives.

You have, to the best of your ability, understood the situation and needs of the people involved. You have felt and acted compassionately.

Again, that is a physical, rather than emotional, example of empathy. You correctly intuited they needed assistance, you called the people that could supply it, and you offered what help you could. You understood the people involved were shaken and hurt. You didn't berate the driver at fault for the accident, you didn't give anyone your opinion on the fact that the corner is a little blind there, and you didn't mention to the passenger in the second car that you didn't like her purse.

Understand? Let's now compare that to sympathy. Sympathy in that example would be you were in the front seat next to the driver. You are in the same situation with the driver and passengers. Now, you are shaken, helpless, and possibly concussed. Can you call for help? Probably not. Your phone went flying out of your hand on impact and is now somewhere in the back seat with a cracked screen. Can you apply pressure to the driver's injury?

Maybe, as soon as your head stops pounding and you can see straight. There's not a lot you can do for the people in the other car since you are trapped by a crushed door in this one. Instead of understanding the situation of the people involved, you are in the accident with them. It makes you less able to help, both in this example and in an emotional setting.

Empathy is the capacity to understand someone's feelings. Sympathy is feeling their feelings with them.

For that reason, when you are having an L2 conversation, it is important to create enough distance between you and the speaker so you understand their feelings, but don't feel their feelings with them.

Empathy is the art and the skill of making the person with whom you are talking feel completely understood by taking their story (their feelings, actions, or thoughts) and showing it back to them, sometimes adding your discernment.

Empathy is not questioning, judgment, opinions or advice.

Empathy is suspending judgment. You are not deciding how you feel about what you are hearing. You are not asking questions taking them off topic. You are making certain the person with whom you are speaking feels understood. They can say what they want or need to say without being interrupted or corrected.

This does not mean you never get to respond, or you are agreeing with what is being said. You will get your chance to respond — just not at this part of the conversation. Does this sound familiar? It should. Empathy is the foundation for RTWYH, responding to what you hear, not what you think about what you hear. If nothing else, I'm consistent.

Concerning advice, here's something none of us really wants to hear. Few people want our advice, though we know ourselves to be quite wise and knowledgeable. People want to be heard much more than they want us to tell them what to do.

Want to be sure about this? Check in with yourself. Think of a time recently when you wanted to talk with someone about an

27

important happening or process in your life, and instead of good, empathetic listening, what you got instead was an earful of advice. Did you like it? Most people don't. If someone wants your advice, they will ask for it. Even then, you might need to think before dispensing any. Is your advice important to this issue, or would it be more beneficial for the person to have to learn about the subject matter and decide for themselves? Perhaps a better role for you is to facilitate the process rather than advise on the answer.

In a church setting, whether a staff member or volunteer, it sometimes feels easy to offer your two cents on someone else's situation. It is possible doing so could be not only counter-productive, but inappropriate. Please, oh, please, understand your role and limits before offering an opinion or advice to anyone, especially in that setting. It can do harm where you would never intend.

Do you know the phrase "We finish each other's sentences?" If someone is finishing someone else's sentences, it's not because they know them so well they can imagine their response. It's because they are interrupting. They're not listening.

For empathy to work, we must change the way we do communication, because so often, our conversations work like this:

You're talking and while that is happening, I'm not really listening, but instead deciding what I'm going to say when you're done (so finish, already) and searching my mind for a story (maybe a better story than the one you're telling) relating to what you're talking about.

Sound familiar? This can happen anywhere — in staff meetings, leading volunteers, handing out food — and all it takes for it to stop is you deciding to make it happen. In any situation, faith-based or otherwise, you can communicate care for the person in front of you by using empathy to understand (rather than experience) their feelings and setting yourself aside in the process. In specific faith-based situations, it would seem imperative to create an arena wherein you are not the focus of the interaction and the assistance you are providing is much more of a one-way street of care to the person being served.

The first thing to check here is your motivation for being there. Working for or serving at a church can have many different purposes. We can absolutely be doing it for God and the Kingdom, but the call to serve can also be part of what we need. It makes us feel good, it can help us to feel obedient to God's request for good works (James 3:17), and we may truly love helping people.

The balance is finding ways to serve that put us in a position to be giving, first and foremost – perhaps receiving something in the mix, but not serving to get something from the people we are trying to help. The time in which we are serving is about them, whether we are fixing a car, preaching, worshiping, or meeting with people in crisis. There are other ways to get the acknowledgement and care we may need. Trying to wrestle it from those you are serving would be like your restaurant server having a seat at your table and asking you to get her a drink and an appetizer. In that situation, it's not the server's needs on the table there (pun intended), but the guest.

If is not part of your serving goal to create a caring, other-focused environment, you've wasted good money on this book. If it is important, read on. There are such appropriate and easy ways to do just that.

6 – The Spotlight

Peppered throughout the Bible are mentions of listening well, combined with the fact we don't need to fill every bit of silence with talk. The book of James is rife with how to treat each other, and as part of the first chapter, the famous "be quick to listen, slow to speak, and slow to get angry" verse is present (James 1:19). The book goes on to talk about "controlling the tongue" (chapter 3), and how judgement is the work of God, not the work of man (chapter 4). Making your way through Proverbs is another good way to understand our role as listeners and speakers.

In any given listening situation, though you have already begun to assess the level (L1 or L2) of a conversation, Active Listening is the first action a speaker will notice about the care you are providing. It pertains to our attitude and behavior while someone else is talking. It is what we're doing while they are speaking, and we are not.

It's all about the spotlight. When you are in a conversation with someone, imagine there is a big spotlight in the room. In a Level 1 or Level 2 talk, when the other person is speaking, the spotlight — the focus and the attention — is on them. When you are talking, the spotlight and attention are on you and they are sitting in the dark.

An L1 talk might well have the spotlight swinging around some. L1 talks tend to be back-and-forth in form, with each person adding to the conversation, but the point remains when the spotlight is on the other person, you are giving them your full attention — not trying to wrestle the light back to yourself. It will be your turn again soon enough.

For the time you spend having an L2 conversation, the spotlight moves around much less. It is still never a monologue, but the fast and easy L1 cadence is rarely present when the importance level goes up. Even when both parties have times they are speaking, there is a calmness to allowing the full spotlight time for each — not grabbing it back, but listening and empathizing until it is your turn again. If the spotlight is swinging around in an L2, it may be someone needs to be quieter. A quick-moving spotlight at that point may indicate one or more people are not giving the needed time for each to be understood. It may be becoming an argument, or someone may be, perish the thought, finishing the other's sentences.

If you see this happening in an L2 conversation and you are the culprit, stop it. Right now. Go back to allowing the full spotlight allotment when the other person is speaking, and respectfully request the same for yourself.

In many faith-based situations, people come to the church for help. In those cases, the time is all about them. This is effort you have given to God's work, to helping others in some way, whether you are a staff member or a volunteer. Time and attention are precious commodities in our culture and to give of yourself well in this way can be a huge blessing to the recipient.

When the other person is speaking, do your best to put aside your own concerns and any judgment to be fully engaged and actively listening. You can't know what someone else is thinking unless you are willing to listen intently — not just for the facts, but for the things simmering underneath, waiting to be said.

Active listening is just that – active. It's not sitting back and waiting to be served information. It is encouraging, sifting through what you're given looking for more, and listening for behaviors and patterns that can help you understand the speaker more completely.

In a church or faith-based organization, it can be difficult to allot the needed spotlight time for a speaker. We often think we know what people need (the Gospel, of course), and can feel quite comfortable cutting them off in the middle of their story to correct and lead them in the right direction. The problem there is hardly anyone comes to Christ by being judged. People come to Christ through love, not a mugging. Listening well doesn't mean agreement, after all, and giving a speaker the time to tell their story and making sure they are understood will go a long way in you (and by association, the church and God) being trusted. I love Proverbs 18:2 that says, "A fool finds no pleasure in understanding, but delights in airing his own opinions."

Active listening is, at its best, both focused and unbiased. Keeping those two words in mind during someone else's spotlight time can keep your tongue and your judgment in check.

To get to the place where you can be attentive without letting yourself get in the way, you need to be in a position to ACT. This is the second acronym.

A – be Accessible
C – be Curious
T – be Tenderhearted

To be **Accessible**, be aware of your current state. If you are preoccupied, judging, angry, or hangry, you will not be at your best in an L2 conversation. Put down the phone, the tablet, and, if appropriate, get a bite to eat. Take off your judge's robes. Pray. Pray for the ability to RTWYH. Then, determine where you are in your head and in your heart. Can you be accessible to the person speaking? If not, what is standing in your way? It could be time, it could be resentment, or it could be a lack of understanding of their situation.

Can you put those issues aside for this time? It will be imperative to not just know what an obstacle to being accessible is, but to dispense with it.

If you can't get accessible, for whatever reason, agree with your conversation partner to wait to talk in order get your head and heart in the right place. As well, they may ask you to wait so they can do the same — sounds reasonable to me. Be careful, however, to not use this as an excuse not to have an important discussion. No dodging allowed under the heading of Accessibility.

Whenever the conversation happens, settle in. Focus your attention. Your accessibility can make the difference between this talk going somewhere or ending before it begins.

Being **Curious** necessitates you not feel you know all there is to know about what will be discussed. To be curious indicates a willingness to learn, both about the speaker and the subject matter. It's a temptation to think talking with the person you sit next to every day or your spouse will net no real revelation. You know them so well.

Here's news. We all change, all the time. We learn new things. We experience situations turning us degrees away from how we used to be. The Holy Spirit speaks, and we are forever transformed. Revelations abound. We are different today than we were yesterday, simply by being alive.

No matter the subject of the talk, being curious allows the speaker to tell you what they know or what they believe to be true. Be willing to hear, to learn. Agreement doesn't have to be part of the deal, but your openness to listen with curiosity will encourage the speaker to be much more open with their thoughts and feelings. You are almost guaranteed to learn something, and in the unlikely event you don't, you have still shown respect and Christ-like attention to the person speaking. Your interruptions to correct facts or insert your opinion can quickly shut down any talk, but especially one starting in, or headed for, L2 territory.

Here's news. Nobody likes a know-it-all. It was true when we were 5, and it's true now. There is little understanding shared when the listener in any conversation has an attitude saying they already know what you are going to say and have already decided what their response is going to be. In a church setting, especially, this can be seen as extra-arrogant – knowing it all about how to fix a car is one thing (though perhaps annoying) but insinuating knowing it all about a person is presumptuous and impossible, all in one. Jesus didn't behave that way, and He did know everything.

Be **Tenderhearted**. This is not kittens and puppies and mushy-gushy feelings. Tenderness can be defined as kindness and gentleness, the treatment Jesus showed to the people with whom he spoke. It is not taking over a conversation. It is being polite and courteous and caring as someone is speaking. It is allowing for compassion to enter any discussion you have.

Courtesy, though not necessarily common, should be rampant in a talk in which there is a reason and the time to listen. Your tenderheartedness will go a long way in the speaker's memories of the conversation and will lay good ground when someone (maybe you!) is asking the same of them.

In any conversation, be ready to **ACT** - be Accessible, Curious, and Tenderhearted.

Next, as a person is speaking, you can be giving them your full attention in concrete ways. The skills we've already discussed can be used anywhere a conversation can take place, be it sitting, standing, in your office, in the hallway, in a car, or in a meeting. Notice I didn't say "sitting in front of a TV/tablet/smartphone" nor "striding down the hallway." Trying to wrestle someone's attention from a device or attempting to keep up with someone as they walk does not create much of an environment to pay attention. It is akin to watching TV and saying over your shoulder, "Yes, I'm listening." It feels dismissive and patently untrue. Not a great start.

To create the best connection, think **POE** (as in quothing the raven). This is the last acronym, I promise.

P – Posture
O – Orientation
E – Eye Contact

P is for **Posture**. Your posture demonstrates your attention when someone is speaking. It is crucial for the speaker to see your intention to listen as they begin to talk.

First, keep your posture open. You may not know what an open posture is, but you sure know what one looks like when it's closed. Imagine someone sitting in front of you while you're talking with their legs crossed and their arms folded across their chest. It is the American classic posture of defensiveness. That would be closed. To be open, loosen up. The rule of thumb is if your legs are crossed, your arms are open — not touching each other and never, ever folded across your chest. If your hands are clasped or touching, then your legs can't be crossed. You get one or the other — not both. As well, try to keep your hands away from your face. Your thoughts and feelings, often expressed by your facial expression, should be accessible to the person with whom you are speaking.

Next, you can show interest in what someone is saying with a slight lean toward them. Notice the word "slight." A deep lean can look creepy or downright menacing. No need to invade someone's personal space. A few degrees will do it.

As much as possible, be (and look) relaxed in your position of either listening or speaking. Sit comfortably attentive. Your look of being at ease may help the other person in the situation be comfortable as well. Slouching is a bit too relaxed, so find a position that isn't awkward. The point here is to try to create the best environment for good communication. You appearing nervous or anxious may encourage the person with whom you are speaking to feel much the same.

The "O" is for "**Orientation**." Be aware of your placement in relation to the person with whom you are talking. As much as humanly possible, sit facing the person as squarely as you can. Some environments won't allow for that, and some take just a bit of adjustment to get there. Face the person speaking. See them and let them see you. Try not to have a significant hindrance between you, like a desk. Some people have their best talks at the dining room table, but try to have it cleared off, and be able to face each other, rather than being at corners sitting on an angle.

The point is to physically see the person with whom you are speaking — their eyes, face, and body language, and to share yours with them. Jesus spent the lion's share of his ministry speaking to people, in their presence, breathing their air. Granted, social media was a long way off, but clearly Jesus valued being with the people He loved and wanted them to be physically close to Him. He spent time in crowds, He had dinner with people, He healed them by touch. Standoffish, He wasn't. The truth that we have technology that can keep us away of everyone, if we choose, doesn't change the fact it is within each other's space, face-to-face, that we will have the best understanding. An exception here is teenagers talking in cars, which seem sometimes to go better when face-to-face speaking isn't possible, but there will be a time to change that so your child doesn't have to ride around in a car for the rest of their lives to have serious discussions.

"**Eye Contact**" is next. Maintaining appropriate eye contact is a standard way to connect. This can be too much of a good thing, as well, so be careful. You're not hypnotizing the speaker — you are showing intentional interest. Keep your look soft, not staring, and make a point of occasionally looking away, but be deliberate about this – enabling good eye contact can help a struggling conversation stay afloat.

American culture is big on eye contact. Other cultures are not. Have awareness with whom you are speaking. If they are not maintaining eye contact, it is not necessarily telling you anything. It is not (don't be silly) proof they are lying, and it is not automatically disrespectful. In many cultures, it is a sign of respect to not keep eye contact. Let us not assume.

In this case, we are offering, rather than requesting, eye contact. Make sure, as the listener, your eye contact is available if the speaker would like it.

Active listening doesn't require much talk from you. You may use a selection of "prompts." They are those nods or monosyllabic noises we make when someone else is talking to get them to talk more (mm-hmm is an ongoing favorite), but for the most part, words don't get used until later. As for nodding, be aware constant nodding makes one resemble a bobblehead doll. Control your prompts, both verbal and non.

Though none of the behaviors of Active Listening are set in our DNA, they all make sense. I haven't said you have to stand on your head or always wear blue when you are performing this skill. I've said to pay respectful attention, face someone who is talking to you, and be curious. There's nothing here that should worry you much, and nothing that will make you argue with me.

I've saved all that for the next chapter.

7 – Ok, Your Turn

"Come to me, all you who are weary and burdened, and I will give you rest. Mt. 11:28

Rest for someone hurting can come in the form of being able to speak freely, without judgement or interruption. This doesn't happen alone, but in company, with a compassionate listener. When the speaker is finished talking, there is more for the listener to do to ensure that rest. It is time for them to speak, and to do it well.

Empathetic Responding is what we do when there is a pause from the person speaking. It is letting them know what you have understood, both about them and the situation, from what they have said. All this Active Listening is for naught if you don't communicate it back. It is taking what you're learned from your Active Listening and presenting it on a platter for the speaker to look at and decide if you are correct in your understanding. Remember from Chapter 5 – empathy is not questions, judgment, opinions, or advice. It is suspending judgment.

People come to the church for all kinds of help on a myriad of different issues and meet with people in a position to listen and assist. For them to feel heard and seen and for the listener to have the pertinent information from which to identify problems and look toward a partnership in solutions, this type of responding is key. It leads to compassionate action. Without this skill both parties in this conversation are flying blind. The guests don't have any clue what the listener knows about them or their story, and the listener doesn't know if they are right or wrong in what they believe to be the guest's perspective. Responding empathetically in this context can show no matter who they are or in what situation they find themselves, they can count on compassion when they turn to the church. It doesn't mean the church will agree or always be able to help, but it does mean the church can always care.

In the beginning, attempting this skill can be a little daunting. Take comfort, however, in knowing in the midst of a conversation, being wrong in your empathy is no big deal. If your speaker disagrees with your assessment of their thoughts and feelings, the good news is they will let you know and give you another shot. It doesn't mean you aren't good at this and should stop trying. It doesn't mean it's just not "you" to be empathetic, and you should go back to being whatever it was you were before. It means you're not a mind reader, or there wasn't enough information for you to empathize more correctly, or you need practice.

To respond empathetically, you will gather information from the Active Listening you did, and, while taking the spotlight off the speaker as little as possible, respond with empathetic statements from <u>their perspective</u>. Notice the underlining, which I hardly ever use. Empathy is about you as the listener making the speaker feel understood. Remember RTWYH – Respond to what you hear, not what you think about what you hear. The goal now is to put together statements from what you believe the speaker is feeling and add pertinent details.

The equation is: Emotion + Situation = Empathy

When someone is speaking, the first thing to look for is the emotion. What is the look on their face? What is their tone of voice? How are they holding their body? You can't depend on the situation deciding what the emotion will be, as we can respond quite differently to the same situation. A job loss for one can be devastating, and to another, liberating. Certainly, don't search in yourself for what you would be feeling in the situation and assume they feel the same.

The speaker will be giving you good clues. Do your best to discern their emotion, and then pair it with the situation at hand.

Here is a tried-and-true formula to get you started:

"You feel {*emotion*} because {*situation*}."

As in:

- "You feel <u>sad</u> because <u>your wife has made it clear she is disappointed with you</u>."
- "You feel <u>excited</u> because <u>you found your dream home</u>."
- "You feel <u>nervous</u> because <u>you feel God is asking you to do something hard</u>."
- "You feel <u>overwhelmed</u> because <u>you have to find a new place to live in two weeks</u>."

When you get more comfortable with this skill, you will instinctively loosen your grip on the formulaic version of empathy, which will make for a more natural sounding conversation. It will also keep your kids from saying, "Don't Dr. Phil me." Examples of less prescribed versions of the above empathy statements might be:

- "<u>Your wife's disappointment</u> makes you <u>sad</u>."
- "<u>Finding your dream home</u> is very <u>exciting</u>!"
- "The fact that <u>God is asking something difficult of you</u> makes you <u>nervous</u>."
- "<u>Having to find another apartment in only two weeks</u> feels <u>overwhelming</u>."

There could be many ways to reword these statements correctly — this is just one example. However you do it, it should still include both emotion and situation, no matter in what order they come.

Emotion + Situation = Empathy.

There may be situations when the first thing you hear is a piece of big news — good or bad. If so, don't launch right into empathy; offer a comment first. It's good manners. If what you're hearing is clearly bad news, "I'm so sorry," is really all that's necessary. You are not commenting on how the bad news is affecting them, because you don't know that yet. You are not giving false hope, as in, "I'm sorry you lost your job, but I'm sure you'll get another one quickly." You are not a prophet. And, hopefully, you are not comparing your experience to theirs. "I'm sorry your house went into foreclosure. I lost my home last year, and it's been the worst time of my life." Can you see the spotlight swinging?

Good news is much the same. A heartfelt, "Congratulations!" without any attempt to pull the conversation away from its original path will get you both quickly back to what the speaker wants to say next, and for now, that's the point.

There may be times when it seems there is no new emotion to pull into the next empathy statement. If there has been a death, it can be the overarching emotion to all the speaker is saying is sadness, but there will be different situations in which the sadness takes on a new form or meaning you can empathize instead of starting every sentence with "You feel sad because..."

An example might be a recent widower telling you seeing a restaurant where he and his wife often ate makes him sad for the meals they won't eat together anymore. Instead of saying, "You feel sad because you can't eat there together anymore," you might say, "Seeing that place recalls what you can no longer share with her."

If it sounds hard, you're right. It can be. Everything worthwhile is hard, right up until you do it well and it's natural instead of contemplated. Like, for instance, walking.

Remember empathy is completely from the speaker's point of view, without your input, agreement, or disagreement. Don't add your opinion on how awful the ex, how ungrateful the boss, or how it will all be all right in the end. When a speaker is talking about an issue with another person, keep in mind you are listening to only one side of a situation. There's a pretty good chance if the other person were there, they might well have a different, though equally strong, opinion on what happened and why. Empathy is not your take on what is said — it is making the speaker feel understood as they are saying it.

Being objective and speaker-focused can get tricky when the speaker is saying something difficult about you. You will have discussions about friction in your own relationships, and the thought of making someone else feel understood while having to empathize your mistakes or faults can take the skill of empathy to an art form. You can do it. It's such a gift to the other person. You can learn to listen and empathize even about yourself. How cool are you?

Nadine – Pastor, I feel like I have to say how much I disagreed with the message last week. I thought you were way off base in your thoughts on how to raise kids. I left feeling very discouraged, and when I looked through my Bible, I couldn't find any reason for what you said.

Pastor – You are unhappy with the contents of the message, and it was discouraging to you as a parent.

Nadine – That's right. I think as parents we have many options on how we want to raise our children, and I don't think your suggestions fit our family.

Pastor – For you, understanding you have choices on how to raise your children is important, and it seemed like I was telling you there was only one option.

Nadine – It did.

Pastor – I'm glad you said something. Please know the suggestions I brought up were just that - only suggestions – not a mandate on how everyone needs to run their families. If you, or you and your husband both, want to stop by the office and talk more about it, I'm happy to do it.

Nadine – Ok. I'll ask him. Thanks for taking the time to talk about it. I feel better.

To begin each empathetic sentence with "I hear you saying that..." or "You feel _____ because _____..." can be boring for you and prescribed for the listener. Here are some examples of different ways to begin an empathetic response statement once you go beyond the beginning empathy equation.

- You are feeling...
- You are saying...
- It sounds like you are...
- That must be...
- This situation must be...
- As you see it,
- You think...
- You believe...
- You see...
- It seems _____ to you.
- It all seems...
- From your perspective...

Wherever you are reading this, I am going to ask you to take a few minutes and do a bit of practice with this concept. It's integral and getting good at it quickly will go a long way in your proficiency.

Please form empathy statements from the following sentences. Start with the formulaic "You feel (emotion) because of (situation)." When you're comfortable with that, do it again in a less prescribed way.

- It made me so mad when the pastor said I wasn't doing my job well. I work hard and stay late almost every night.

  Formula _____

  _____

  Non- Formula _____

  _____

- My girlfriend says if I don't quit drinking, she's going to break up with me. Whatever. I can't stand her nagging me all the time.

  Formula _____

  _____

  Non- Formula _____

  _____

- My parents don't want me to move away, but this is a great opportunity. I'm sorry to disappoint them, but I'm going to take the job.

  Formula _____

  _____

  Non- Formula _____

- I'm worried you won't help me because I don't go to this church. I wouldn't have come, but I'm desperate.

Formula _____

_____

Non- Formula _____

_____

- I really hate it when you cut me off when I'm talking. It makes me feel like you don't care about what I'm saying.

Formula _____

_____

Non- Formula _____

_____

How are you doing? Keep going if you can. If not, take a break before completing the rest of these.

- It feels like when I come to the Food Pantry, some of the people treat me like I shouldn't be here. I feel really judged.

Formula _____

_____

Non- Formula _____

_____

- I really don't like my daughter's small group leader. I think she's advising her against our family values.

  Formula _____

  _____

Non- Formula _____

_____

- When we moved in with my husband's parents, I didn't realize they expected us to have every meal with them. It's a little too much "family time" for me.

  Formula _____

  _____

Non- Formula _____

_____

- I wish I could love the new assistant pastor. Maybe I'll get used to how he preaches, but it's hard for me now.

  Formula _____

  _____

Non- Formula _____

_____

- With our church in upheaval, it's hard to worship. I'm not sure what to believe.

    Formula _____

_____

    Non- Formula _____

_____

Empathic Responding. It's the tool you can't put down. It creates an arena of understanding and trust. Once mastered, you will use it in nearly every conversation. It's even better than one of those screwdrivers fitting every screw, and hardly anything is better than that.

8 – Not an Interrogation

If you enjoy listening and are getting better at Care Talk with every chapter, the next obvious thing would be to ask some good questions, right? You need more information and what better way to get it than with a barrage of questions. In the biz, we call these "probes," and I'm sorry to say as someone is telling you a story, needing to be understood, or ranting and raving, you as the listener need to significantly limit your probes.

Here's something you may have never considered (but you will now). Every time you ask a question, it changes the course of the conversation. Every time. For example, if you come to tell me you've been downsized, and the first thing I say is, "Have you updated your resume?" the telling of the story has now ended and we are on to other things.

Play this out some more. If you tell me you rented a new apartment, and I say, "Will your huge couch fit?," you don't get to tell me how excited you are to be closer to work, or it's both cheaper and bigger than your current apartment, or now I get to pick you up on my way to work every day. I have cut you off from what you wanted to say in order to take measurements on your couch.

When someone starts talking, they usually have an agenda on what they want to convey. They have a subject and subheadings to cover — apartment, location, cheaper and bigger. You breaking in with a question not fitting their agenda sidetracks what the speaker wants to say. Be patient. You will have a chance to ask questions — just not at the front end of the conversation. For now, let the speaker set the agenda, and you listen and empathize. When they got to the part about the new apartment being cheaper and bigger, your question would have been answered on its own, without you butting in.

If someone comes to the church for financial help, part of what they want to do is tell you their story. They want you to know how they got to where they are, that there were reasons that made sense to them. They want you to know they are not inept. Every action has a decision-making process, and the person sitting in front of you asking for help wants you to understand theirs. If you don't let the story be told, if you interrupt and say what should have happened, the insurance bill might get paid, but the speaker will not feel cared for by you, or, in the larger context, by the church. Not good.

It is common, both in casual conversation and within many arenas in the church, to move very quickly from someone bringing up an issue to problem solving. Imagine going to a doctor. You walk in and say, "My hand hurts." Dr. Insta-Fix, instead of letting you tell him or her about the nature of the pain, when you fell on it, and what happened to create that huge scrape on your knuckles, puts a Band-Aid on it and gives you a lecture on not fighting anymore. Next patient, please! My guess is you would not return.

Imagine a conversation being a road. What the speaker wants to talk about is like starting down that road. The road might curve here and there, because not every conversation is a straight line. When you ask a question, you are taking a turn off the road onto a side street. It's possible the side street leads into a labyrinth of other side streets, and it may be hard to find your way back to the main road. Sometimes the side street is a dead end, and the conversation stops right there, stalled in an area of town where the speaker never meant to be. Even if you get back to the main road, it may take some time to get your speed back up to the original subject matter. Ask another question and away you fly again — veering off to the right or the left, but not where the speaker intended to go.

Questions can also quickly become an interrogation (like the bare lightbulb in the dark room), and now the conversation is completely in your control, with the speaker just there to supply you with the information you want, but not able to talk about what they were intending. Speakers, as a rule, aren't crazy about that.

When the time comes to ask questions, there's a right way to do it. You may need questions as the talk progresses, for clarification or to move things along, but there are clear ways not to make the turns that take the conversation completely off course and mired in a subdivision of streets named after 18th century poets.

Here are the Care Talk rules regarding questions:

First, don't ask two questions in a row. No one likes to feel interrogated, and as you now know, asking a question changes the course of the conversation. If you have a question to ask, get the answer and provide some empathy and attention to it before moving on.

Second, make sure the questions are for the good of the speaker or to get basic clarification, as in, "Wait, I'm confused. That was your mother's plumber's brother-in-law's boss?" Questions simply to satisfy your own curiosity should wait. No need to risk changing the path of what the speaker wants to say just to feed your insatiable need for detail. When the telling of the story is done, or when the speaker feels understood and respected, feel free to go back and feed that beast, but for now, the questions that are worthwhile are the ones helping the speaker stay on track.

Some things just aren't fair. The third rule is in that camp. In a conversation such as the ones we are discussing, never ask a "Why" question. For whatever reason, asking a question starting with the word "Why" denotes disapproval. Let's try it out. Pretend I say to you, "Why did you wear that shirt today?" What might you assume I felt about your shirt? You would assume I didn't like it or disapproved with your choice of shirts. In a broader sense, there can be no good answer for a "Why" question. When your boss asks, "Why is the paperwork not finished?" he or she isn't usually asking why the paperwork isn't finished. They are usually expressing disapproval about the paperwork not being finished.

The effect on the "Why-ee" is typically defensiveness. If I feel disapproval from you, about my clothing choice or my work habits, I will often stand up for myself. Most people's first reaction is not to question the disapproval, but to defend their position. This will certainly be true of someone sitting in front of you asking for assistance from the church. The more "why" questions you ask, the more judged and defensive they will feel.

As a parent, I wish I could retroactively change my wording every time I looked at my kids, from birth until I learned this valuable rule, and said, "Why did you do that?" I was not asking for a flowchart of their thought process leading up to the event. I was making clear I disapproved with their choice of action but hiding it with a question to which there was no good answer. These were Bad Mom Moments.

For the scientists, engineers, inventors, and creators of all ilk, nothing might happen without asking "why" questions – "Why doesn't this work well?" gets things fixed, "Why is this blue perfect with that gray?" changes a line of spring clothing. "Why can't we go to the moon?" put me in front of a TV in 1969, amazed. The "whys" in science are much different than the "whys" in relationships. Even so, scientists beware – how you ask your "whys" might get you even better results.

In relationships, however, "why" questions can be more philosophical than useful, and there is rarely a good answer for them. Mostly, they simply convey disapproval for an action, occurrence, or thought.

- Why did you do that?
- Why me?
- Why did you get the light brown sugar instead of the dark brown?
- Why did you leave your (shoes, purse, keys, mail, coffee cup, armadillo) there?
- Why aren't you listening?

- Why haven't you (left, arrived, fed the armadillo)?
- Why won't you (get a job, quit drinking, start exercising, move over)?

Sometimes you will need to get "why" information without actually asking a "why" question. This is not as tricky as it sounds. You can easily reword the sentence to begin with a different interrogative choice. Before you ask, you cannot replace "Why did you do that?" with "What were you thinking?", though it is suggested in every workshop I've ever taught. You can, however, replace "Why did you do that?" with "What led up to your decision?" It just sounds and feels different.

Here is a list of questions you can use sparingly that won't drive the conversation into another state, and can get information about the speaker you might need to better understand them.

- How did you feel about what happened?
  This is great when someone is storytelling or giving you a lot of facts, but you are not hearing much emotion about a situation.
- What were the results of the situation?
  This is helpful to move from the telling of a story to what happened as a result. Nothing wrong with a good story, but it's important to hear the implications of the situation in order to know how the speaker has been impacted.
- What is most concerning about this issue?
  This brings to focus what is bothering the speaker most. Some stories will be complicated and have many components causing pain or discomfort. You need to know what is bubbling to the top.

You can also use the time-honored "Help me understand…" to begin a sentence as long as you don't use a "why" in the middle.

At this point, you are still just reflecting what the person has said so you can be certain you understand and can communicated understanding back to the them in an empathetic form. Don't forget RTWYH – it's still not what you think about what you're hearing.

A tidbit to remember is we all tend to put ourselves in the best possible light when relating a story or situation. Think of a story you've told in the last few days where you were, even by an inch, a better guy than the other one in the story. We believe ourselves to be in the right most of the time or we wouldn't have done what we did, right? We tell the story from our perspective with us in the right, and the other guy, even a nice guy, just a little more wrong.

For this reason, it is not necessary to believe every word you are hearing from the speaker's perspective. It is only necessary to make certain you understand it and to be able to communicate understanding to the speaker. You will get your chance to disagree, if needed, and quite respectfully, later.

9 – The Crying Side of Town

Here's the deal — people cry. It's not just for little girls. Jesus cried. Some people cry every time they see a puppy video or a soldier surprising his or her children by coming home early. Of course, other people would rather have their appendix out than cry and take great pains (in stony silence) to make sure no one sees them in that delicate condition. For someone coming to the church in a crisis or for help, tears are often a part of the conversation.

It's important to note tears don't always mean the situation is extreme. Some people, as they tell me in their first therapy session, are "criers." Men will more often say, "I'm emotional," but it means the same thing. They show emotion with tears. It's part of who they are.

When you are having a conversation with someone and they start to cry, what is your usual response? Are you fine, slightly uncomfortable, or breaking out in hives? Whatever your reaction internally, it would probably be good to have a few go-to's on how to behave externally.

If someone is crying in your presence, it is not your job to make them stop. Your job in those moments is to be of appropriate comfort. Be willing to be present, not embarrassed or looking like you're sitting on a pinecone, with an empathetic look on your face. Give them their time. You can do this without feeling pressured to fix the problem, and you can do this without touching them. Not everyone who cries wants a hug, and you can be of strong comfort right from your own chair.

When most people cry, it is a release of emotion, not a new career. People don't usually cry for very long. A few minutes of tears is usually the extent of it and your willingness to stay in the room, both figuratively and literally, can offer the support they need to go on.

It is not usually necessary to say much when someone is actively crying. To talk over someone's tears is usually more for the watcher, as they feel like they should be doing something, and what comes to mind is talking the crier out of crying. Saying things like, "It will be all right," or "I'm sure you'll get a new job soon," does less to comfort the crier than to give the watcher a job. As well, you have no idea if either of those comfort-sounding sentences are true, so better to hold your piece and wait it out.

Here's your job: Let the crier cry in your presence, knowing they are neither judged nor ridiculed, and be tender in the process. I say this like it's easy. It is not. We want to fix things. We want whoever is crying to not be so sad.

Unfortunately, the situation is often not ours to fix, so here is what you can do. Be fully present, with a soft look on your face, and be kind. Wait gently for them to be finished.

Here is what not to do. If someone is crying, do not grab ten tissues out of the box and shove them in their hand. As helpful as it might seem in the moment, what is actually conveyed is "Whoa! I am very uncomfortable with your tears. Could you please mop it up?" Certainly, have tissues available, especially in situations where they are likely to be needed, and place them close enough to be reached. A person crying, with the usual accompaniment of a running nose and wet face, will get a tissue when they are ready and without your assistance.

It's possible the tears feel manipulative to you. No need to fall for that, either. By using the skills outlined, you can maintain the separation discussed previously so you are understanding the crier's feelings, but not feeling their feelings with them. Again, no one cries all day. Preserving your boundaries and composure will make it much more difficult for someone trying to manipulate you with their tears. You can empathize with someone's tears while not letting those same tears make your decisions for you.

It may never be easy to watch someone cry but understanding your role can make the experience less traumatic for you both.

10 – It Really Isn't About You

It's time to talk about self-disclosure. What I'm going to say is counter-cultural and contrary to popular opinion, but quite true nonetheless.

In most conversations, whether L1 or L2, it is not helpful for the person speaking to hear your story and how it relates to their situation. Against what is often thought, it does not create a bond with the speaker or help them in their current issue. It just takes the spotlight off them and puts it on you. Even in a lighthearted L1 talk, having someone cut you off when you are telling a funny story in order to tell theirs is swinging the spotlight in a way you would not appreciate.

Here is a conversation that should never happen between my friend Terry, who recently lost his mom, and me.

Shannon – Terry, I'm so sorry about your mom.

Terry – Thank you. We knew she was getting worse, but we thought we would have more time than this.

Shannon – Oh, I know. When my mom got sick, they told us she had 18 months, and she died in three weeks.

Terry – Well, it wasn't quite like that, but she did go faster than we expected. She had dementia, too, so I'm not sure how much she realized about how sick she was.

Shannon – My mom didn't have dementia, but at the end, she was on painkillers and wasn't aware of her surroundings. I know just how you feel.

Terry – Well, I think she's at peace now, anyway.

Shannon – My mom, too. We were glad in the end it went quickly without any pain. So, I just wanted to say how sorry I am about your loss.

Can you hear me grabbing the spotlight and dragging it around to myself? All I've done is take the focus off Terry's loss and shine it on mine. Nothing I said in that awful made-up conversation can be helpful to Terry. I'm not showing compassion for his family, any interest in how he's doing, or honoring his mom in any way.

It gets worse. Everything I said gave the impression I knew all about what Terry was feeling because I had felt something similar with my mom. Really?

There are few relationships more complicated than parents and children. Look at Jesus and his parents! To assume all our losses fit into the same box is ridiculous. When my mom died and since, it has been very clear my sisters and I all had different relationships with her, miss different things, and were annoyed by different habits. To assume I understand their experience concerning my mom's death is plainly incorrect - and we share blood. For me to believe I understand Terry's feelings and reactions to his mom's death without him expressly telling me borders on science fiction.

Another thing my evil twin seems to be saying is, "Oh, I know all about that. No need to say any more — clearly our situations are much the same, and I have all that information already."

A speaker in a conversation like that can walk away feeling confused. They don't feel heard or understood, but they may not be certain what went wrong. People who are aware of this concept walk away angry or annoyed.

When my graduate students hear this lecture, they often respectfully argue with me. They feel it creates a connection when situations are compared. I tell them the same thing I'm going to tell you. Try it out. For the next week, pay attention to when this happens to you and see how it feels. See how you like it when someone insinuates they "know just how you feel," because they have been part of a similar (or not-so-similar) situation. Feel understood? Feel validated? I think not. Try talking to someone who responds to everything you say with the phrase, "I know," indicating their information on all you are thinking and feeling is complete. I have ten bucks saying you're not going to like it.

Even simply indicating you have experienced something similar is not helpful. It still twists the spotlight away, and then assumes your experience is somehow related to the speakers in a way that is helpful. It is not usually the case.

There may come a time when the telling of your experience is wanted or needed. You'll know that time, because the speaker will ask for it specifically, as in, "How did you manage holidays when you lost your mom? I don't know what I'm going to do when Christmas comes." Even then, it is not advice the speaker is looking for, but rather your take on a situation, which in the end may or may not be helpful.

It is also incorrect to assume you can help someone better in a situation because the same thing has happened to you. Often, your thoughts, emotions, and personal circumstances can get in the way of completely understanding someone else's. RTWYH continues to be important (Respond to what you hear, not what you think about what you hear). Empathy is about objectivity, not shared experience.

Here is why we don't want this chapter to be true. We would like self-disclosure to be helpful because we like telling our stories. We like to feel what we experienced (or the fun of telling it) will be illuminating and empowering to someone listening — they will learn something from what happened to us and be better in some way. This is possible, of course. We learn from other people all the time. It just usually doesn't happen in the same conversation as someone sharing their thoughts or feelings with you.

There are venues where sharing similar stories is the whole point. Addiction recovery meetings, grief groups, and other self-help groups are based on people telling and listening to stories. There can be comfort and healing among a group of people who have experienced similar situations and can talk about it together.

Even in those groups, however, a facilitator is usually there to monitor the spotlight, seeing each person gets their time and the attention. This, too, can be done badly. I have had clients pay for a session to talk about how a group leader talked about themselves for most of the time and then wondered why there was not more engagement with the rest of the participants.

If you feel you have an inspiring story and want other people to learn from it, become a public speaker. Do TED Talks. Join Toastmasters. Don't assume every conversation is the perfect place to share all you know and have learned when the person speaking is simply trying to be understood.

You can, however, use your knowledge and experience to empathize more completely. Remembering how you felt in a given situation may give you a leg up on finding the perfect words to use in an empathy statement.

A better version of me in the earlier conversation with Terry would be:

Shannon – Terry, I'm so sorry about your mom.

Terry – Thank you. We knew she was getting worse, but we thought we would have more time than this

Shannon – It was surprising, then, that she passed away so quickly.

Terry – It was. We expected her to live another year at least. She had some dementia, as well, so we don't really know if she understood how sick she was or if she knew we were all there with her.

Shannon – It must have been so hard for you to not know whether she knew the end was close or could feel your care for her.

Terry – It really was. I think once we get past her birthday it will ease up some, but right now it's really painful.

Shannon – Did you mention to me at some point your mom was big on Christmas?

Terry – Yes, that's right, she was. Come to think of it, Christmas will be even harder than her birthday. I hadn't thought of that. Maybe we can plan something special to do as a family.

Shannon – I hope it all goes well. Again, I'm so sorry. My best to your family. We are praying for you all.

Terry – Thank you.

This was not a huge deal. I didn't fix any problems and I didn't perform the service. I did bring food, but that's what you do. For our brief time, I just let Terry talk about his mom without barging in. It didn't change his life, but it didn't make him mad either — probably a best-case scenario for any sad situation.

In churches, it is very common for people to volunteer in a ministry where care has been given to them. For that reason, people can often assume the experience they had relates to everyone else's experience in the same arena, whether it's the loss of a loved one, a job, needing to use the food pantry, or being the parent of twins. At a very top-level view, it can increase your capacity for empathy, but digging down into the actual experience, it can quickly move to sympathy or the forum for constant self-disclosure. If you are serving in a ministry where you have had personal experience, it will be very important to put yourself aside when you are with the people being served. You each have your own very personal experiences relating to the subject at hand. Even though they may fit into the same category, everyone's journey is their own. Please make certain your goal for serving is not to have a new audience for your story, but to use the care you received as motivation to serve others with a similar thorn in their side.

As much as we would like to think it, our experiences are not a best-practice manual for everyone else. Just because something worked for us doesn't mean it will work for them and forcing the spotlight away from a person speaking about something important will hardly encourage them to tell you more. To have and build a relationship or convey empathy and understanding, it is imperative to provide a non-competitive arena in which someone else can talk without us interjecting ourselves at every opportunity. At its worst, a conversation like that becomes simply a silent skirmish for the spotlight, with both people struggling for it until one or the other just gives up.

We can all do better than that

11 – Say It With An "R."

Let's face it. There will instances when you can't have whatever conversation is trying to take place. You might not have the time, or you may not be the correct person with whom to have it. You may have to decide if the conversation will ever take place.

For our purposes, when there is the inability or lack of want to have a particular conversation, you can reach for one of the 3 R's — Refer, Reschedule, or Refuse.

First, are you the right person to be listening to this matter? If this is a question or issue that is not yours to handle, you may need to Refer. Not even Jesus did everything. In Mark 6:7, He sent the disciples out to help in His work, telling to teach and giving them authority over evil spirits. Referral at work.

It is important to still show empathy in the moment of the request for your attention, but it may then need to be handed off to someone who can manage the problem or request. For example:

"You are concerned about the care being given to your child by a particular volunteer. I want to make sure you speak with the right person to get your needs addressed. Can I put you in touch with the manager of that age group? I will let her know to expect your call."

Then, make sure you do exactly that. Shoot off an email or a text, let the manager know what you heard, and, to the best of your ability, get them connected. To be properly empathetic but fall short in the execution of what you've promised will throw high-octane gas on an already lit fire and will make the ensuing talk with the manager so much worse. Follow up.

Notice, too, the presence of RTWYH in the response. You are not agreeing with their assessment, arguing with their premise, or defending the organization. You are reflecting the speaker's position and referring them to the person who can address their concerns.

Occasionally, Refer gets used as a dodge — a nicely worded version of "I don't want to deal with that even though it's mine to do." Passing the buck can be costly in terms of wasted time and effort and can be harmful to the passer's reputation. This remains true for the proverbial "Don't ask me, ask Mom," or "Check with your Dad — I'm busy." If it's an honest Referral, great. If it is a way to have someone else make the decision so you divest yourself of responsibility but can still complain about the result — bad form.

Next, is this a conversation that is yours to have, but you can't have it now? You may need to Reschedule for a future time, while still making the person feel heard in the moment.

"You have ideas on how we can get more fresh food for the food pantry. I want to hear about this, but I'm on my way to a meeting and won't be free until after 2:00. Can we meet after that? How about 2:15?"

Most people don't mind having something Rescheduled if it means being able to have the full conversation. Rescheduling can badly backfire if the meeting is not kept, or if it was a way to show disrespect or powering-up in terms of whose time is more important. ("I'll have the meeting, but I'll make you wait for it.") The point of a Reschedule is to give the speaker the full attention they deserve and keep you as the listener intent on your job — listening and understanding.

Another example might be:

"Maria, I'm completely beat. I want to hear what you have to say, but I'm totally on empty and don't think I can be a good listener until I get some rest. Can we please have this talk first thing in the morning? I'll make the coffee."

Some situations dictate the conversation requested is just not going to take place. In these cases, you may have to Refuse. For some people, not getting the answer they wanted is cause for trying again and again. Whether in a work or volunteer situation, or in a decision you have made with your child, revisiting the matter several times without change can end up with frustration and resentment on both sides — one side still angry about the decision made, and the other frustrated with the failure to accept it.

There can be other reasons you may need to Refuse, but the result will be the same. Some discussions need to be closed. I encourage you to be careful before using Refuse, however. Within reason, make certain there is nothing left to be said. Depending on the situation, you may still have an ongoing relationship with the other person involved, and to Refuse prematurely can be difficult on your connection. By the same token, to not use a Refuse when it is clearly needed can let a poor situation drag on interminably.

Breakups of all kinds happen for a reason. As a therapist, I hear stories of breakups with people, jobs, and circumstances. How much talking is enough? When is resolution reached? There is no easy answer, but it is a good question to ask yourself and the other involved as you go. At some point, more discussion about a situation that is not going to change can create an unhealthy pattern for both parties.

It is a delicate balance, and not one easily found. There can be pain involved. The only good news is the person being Refused can still feel your care even while having their request denied.

"You are frustrated that the church will not help you financially right now. I'm sorry for your frustration, but this is not a matter that is going be opened up for discussion again. Is there any way I can help you to move on from here?"

A personal situation might sound like this:

"I know you are unhappy with my decision. I'm sorry we can't find agreement on this. I don't think it's helpful for either one of us to go over it again and again. Our relationship is important to me (only say this if it is). What can I do to help us move on from here?"

Just because there are issues with no clear resolution or agreement doesn't mean the relationship needs to suffer forever. "Agree to disagree" has been around for a long time, and how you present the thought that no amount of talking will change your mind on a given subject can be the path by which the relationship is repaired, restored, or renewed.

I may be overusing that letter a bit today.

Refer, Reschedule, Refuse — all tools to make someone feel heard and understood when you can't, or won't, engage.

12 – Under Cover

Discernment is the thing that happens when you are listening to someone and you get a little spiritual poke. Not a physical poke, but a mental one. Your ears come to a point, you pay even closer attention, and a thought forms you didn't have before, like, "I think the student pastor's irritation with not being able to find the list from Costco has more to do with last week's low attendance than the available snack choices."

The definition of discernment is being able to grasp and comprehend what is hidden or obscure. In the Bible, one of the words used is "diakrisis," which means to be able to distinguish or appraise a person, statement, situation, or environment.

Discernment means being able to unearth and bring to the surface what is uncertain. In a conversation, this can have many presentations. Like the example above, you can have a flash of intuition or jolt of understanding making perfect sense out of something not quite clicking.

Upon asking someone smarter than me to do Biblical research on this word and its construct, it turns out there are many words in the Bible for discernment, meaning a variety of different things. They include, in no particular order:

1. The understanding of good and evil
2. Knowing the difference between wisdom and folly
3. To investigate
4. To watch with a goal of understanding God's will
5. To judge

For listening and understanding, we will use all the definitions of discernment except #5, Judging. As before mentioned, judging doesn't have a place in empathy, so we will leave that to

God and juries, of which we are neither. Though it may be necessary in the church for someone to suffer consequences for their behavior, it's not the same as judging them. Consequences usually come as a necessity to protect someone or something and can be done without judging, which Biblically, is God's domain alone.

That being said, we can use discernment to help people, to protect the church, and to know when to speak and when to take a big ol' glass of Shut the Heck Up. The verse coming to mind is Proverbs 2:2 – "...turning your ear to wisdom, and your heart to understanding."

The Bible also says in Psalm 19:12, "Who can discern his errors? Please forgive my hidden faults," seeming to say for all our personal introspection, we are not fully able to see the complete picture of ourselves and need others to help. It is that concept we can use for another's gain when discernment about them is present.

On the plane going on vacation a few years ago, a friend and I took a fun personality test I use in my practice. We went over the questions when we were done and argued with each other on some of the answers. She disagreed with me on how I had answered some of them, and me, her. In some cases, we had been too hard on ourselves, and other times not quite as accurate as the other thought was possible. After discussion, we both had a better idea of who we were not only from the inside looking out, but to someone with a front row seat to our personalities and behaviors.

Shadowed in our stories and lives are our motivations, strengths and weaknesses, and values and priorities. The more you know about someone, the more likely your discernment will be true, because the more foundational information you have, the more your subconscious will put together.

In a church setting, it is seeing more than someone has said. It helps us see needs someone hasn't verbalized and patterns of behavior making it hard for them to change. It can be old hurts and wounds that are not healed, and a glimpse at what someone is hiding. This is how it can work:

You are listening to someone's story and providing lots of RTWYH. As you are listening, some things have stuck out to you, whether it seems to be a contradiction in the story or a piece that's missing. Something is nudging you; a thought or a feeling saying, "Hey, ask about the situation from a few years ago," or "She never mentions her mom in this story. I wonder why."

The kicker about discernment is there is no guarantee. You could well be wrong with a perceived insight and therefore not discerning at all. It happens all the time.

Sometimes, our snarky little mind makes stuff up and tries to pass it off as discernment. We add what we think about the person or the situation and it tries to come out as being insightful when it's really judgmental. It takes a bit to realize when that is happening but the more experience you have, the easier it is to separate when it's your take on something or actual discernment. The great part is you can easily find out if you're right.

There is no question who the expert is on the person across from you in a room. As much as we would love to think we "know them better than they know themselves," it is blatantly not true, and a bit of an insult. The fact we may be able to see a blind spot in someone does not make us the reigning authority on all things "them." They know most of their thoughts, feelings, and behaviors. We know what we can see, what we're told, and what we can discern. We are woefully underequipped to call ourselves fully informed, much less the expert. We are, in fact, not God.

If we want to know if we are discerning, we can find out. Ask the person to whom the potential discernment refers. They will either confirm or deny what you think, and your thoughts can be used or discarded at their discretion, whether true or not. In some instances, they might disagree, they might not be able to stand the insight now, or you might be wrong, but be careful before offering your comments. There are no "takebacks" after the words are spoken.

Your discernment is only as good as the help it can provide the person to whom it is offered. It is not proof of your worth. Your discernment is a potential gift to the other person involved, not a badge for you to wear.

Think of discernment like a birthday gift. Some gifts you took out of the box, put on, and used consistently from that moment until now. Some gifts were not really to your liking, and got used only sporadically, if at all. Some gifts went from your hand right to the donate pile or got re-gifted. Then, there is the gift you didn't need when you received it — it didn't fit, or it wasn't useful until a specific situation arose. Then, when you pulled it out later, it was perfect and useful and beautiful, and you were grateful to have it.

This is how discernment goes. Some is instantly useful, some not so much, and some gets put away for later. Whatever the receiver decides to do with it is their choice. Like a birthday gift, it is no longer yours to decide once it leaves your hand.

And, don't forget, you can be so very wrong. Just like the total miss on a gift, your discernment can be off base, the wrong size or style, and rejected out of hand.

Delivery is huge. To launch discernment at someone like a fastball over home plate can make it difficult for the hearer to accept. This is a suggestion, not required consumption. Behave like a host or hostess offering a warm drink. It is a question, not a command. The host says, "Would you care for coffee?" not "Drink the coffee I made for you."

Discernment is offered in the same way. It comes out as, "I'm wondering about your mom. You haven't mentioned her in this story. Was she involved?" as opposed to "Your mother abandoned you, didn't she?"

A gentler entrance can leave the hearer time to consider, time to think. They can accept your premise or disagree. That's their right as the expert.

In a variety of ministry settings, staff and volunteers often speak to someone coming to the church for the first time or to people they don't know intimately. Most care-related help is, by design, given by people not knowing the recipient well, to keep the process objective. Intuiting and using discernment must be with that knowledge – you don't know this person well and your discernment can certainly be wrong. It doesn't mean you don't pay attention to it. It does mean your presentation is careful and cautions.

Let's say you are positive you are right in your discernment, and the person listening won't accept it. What to do? Imagine how it would play out in a pastoral care meeting.

Diana – As we've talked, I've been thinking about what you said concerning Dan's part in the house being lost to foreclosure. Is it possible you are still angry about that?

Stella – No, I don't think so. I think I've forgiven him, even though it was the gambling that really caused it all to come crashing down.

Diana – Are you sure? I hear a lot of anger there, down deep. I really think I'm right about this.

Stella – I think you're mistaken. We have talked about it a lot, Dan and I, and I really think I've come to terms with what each of our parts was in the process.

Diana – I would think about it more. I'm pretty sure you are still quite angry.

Stella – I've already said I think you're wrong. Can we drop it?

Diana – Ok, but promise me you'll think about it.

Stella – I won't. I know my relationship a lot better than you do, and I know you're wrong. I'm not discussing it again.

It would seem Diana was either certain in her idea or gets some validation out of being right in her discernment. Either way, she put Stella off to the extent she would be hard-pressed to ever bring that subject up in discussion again. As opposed to this:

Diana – As we've talked, I've been thinking about what you said concerning Dan's part in the house being lost to foreclosure. Is it possible you are still angry about that?
Stella – No, I don't think so. I think I've forgiven him, even though it was the gambling that really caused it all to come crashing down.
Diana – Hmmm. I thought I sensed some anger. Is there someone else that comes to mind?
Stella – Well, I am still angry at the mortgage company. They first said they would help us with a refinance, and then reneged and refused any help at all. When I think about the foreclosure, that's who I'm mad at.
Diana – Ok, how the mortgage company acted is what really made you mad in this situation.
Stella – You bet. I probably still blame them, even though it was mostly our fault it all happened. I know it doesn't help me to be mad at a whole company. I should probably let it go.

Diana wasn't wrong about the anger. She was wrong about the recipient. It does not help to try and argue a speaker into believing your discernment or empathy. They are the most knowledgeable on whatever situation is being discussed. Believe them. If in fact your discernment is correct and, for whatever reason, they don't see it or can't accept it, it might be the gift tucked in the back of the closet until they decide it's needed — when it fits, or when it's useful.

Discernment is never about "catching" the other person doing something wrong. It is about bringing something out of the shadows when it can be of better use in the light.

There are some practical steps for being in the best place to access and use discernment.

- Pray. The best discernment is of the Holy Spirit and asking Him into any situation early is a great start.
- Be in good shape yourself. What keeps your mind clear? Provide good self-care, like rest, eating well, and exercise.
- Know and understand the boundaries you have with any one person. It is not always appropriate to share your discernment. Not every relationship is the same.
- Having discernment about a situation still doesn't mean you get to give advice. What is your role in this situation or relationship? Be very clear on that and very careful before offering advice.
- If there is discernment you have uncovered that may be difficult for the other person to hear, present it in a caring, respectful way. You are never judge and jury.
- Couch your comments with consideration. Using phrases like, "I'm confused about..." or "Is it possible that..." not only allow for you to be wrong, it gives the person speaking the space to discuss the issue at hand.

The point of discernment is to be helpful to the other person. Sometimes, the most helpful thing you can do is be quiet. Part of discernment is deciding whether to share it. There are other times when a person can be in such crisis or confusion when your discernment can help them make sense of something difficult and give words to their pain.

Either way, the goal is to have the action you take be strictly for the good of the other person. That is discernment in action, and it is fabulous to behold.

13 – Those Darn Kids

Children are a special population in so many ways, whether you connect with them at church or at home, but what seems clear from birth is kids will most often do what they see and recreate what they know. Communication is no exception. If children are part of an environment where they are listened to and their words are respected, they will be much more likely to give those same allowances in other relationships. The other side of the coin is not as shiny. If children experience an inability from the adults in their lives to hear and consider what they are saying, they will be much more likely to drag that into their future, recreating a communication system where rules are confusing and getting attention or understanding depends on volume and intensity rather than innate regard.

In a church setting, from birth to high school, the question becomes how to respect and encourage honest talk from the child in order to teach, protect, and encourage them on their bumpy way to Christian adulthood.

Some of it can be quite the sticky wicket. As either staff or volunteer, you are not the parent, and deciding what to say, do, and share is cause for consternation and many, many meetings on behalf of children's and student ministries everywhere. This book is not in any way a manual on how to set up student ministry, but making clear the construct on how to talk to kids, and how to encourage them to talk to you. It begins with questions.

- What is the goal of this ministry?
  - Is the ministry set up to encourage discussion between kids and volunteers or staff, or is it a listening-only forum? If there is any back and forth conversation, please make sure that staff and volunteers are trained to do their best in those

situations where kids are talking about things important to them.

- What are the responsibilities and boundaries of this ministry?
  - o Student leaders, whether staff or volunteer can make a huge difference in a child or teenager's life. If people have had a great student leader, they are often remembered by name for the rest of the student's existence. A student leader, however, does not take the place of a family, and the talking between the student and leader should still fall well within the boundaries set by the ministry. A volunteer leader is not usually a therapist or pastor, and should not try to fill those shoes.
- Is there a difference between what a staff member and a volunteer would do or say?
  - o Unless there is a specific situation where this would change, staff and volunteers should be trained and perform quite similarly to each other so the kids can know what to expect. Staff might have more in the way of resources to encourage or give, but the same skills and boundaries would usually be the same for them both.
- When should a volunteer report a conversation to staff?
  - o Nearly all who come in within breathing distance to kids are labeled as "mandatory reporters." If you don't, as staff or volunteer, know what that is, please find out. It is the law on what you are required to report and has to do with protection of the students from themselves or others. Danger must be reported, not just to staff, but to authorities or parents. Most churches will have a set legal standard on how to take these very important steps. If your church does not, there is

work to be done to protect not just the student but the church.

The earlier you teach and model good communication skills with the kids with whom you come in contact, the better. The great news is it is never too late to start. You are going to use the same skills no matter when and how you begin. Empathy is empathy, no matter the age of the recipient, and the joy for both of you of being able to accurately determine and reflect the thoughts and feelings of the other can only make your connection, at home or at church, better.

Starting small — not small efforts, but with small people — will include all the acronyms we've had so far – RTWYH, ACT, and POE.

Shrinking skilled communication down to pint-size is no different than grinding up your food so kids can eat it. It's smaller in size, less in amount, and it's usually simpler, without the sauces or spices we use to make our adult food more interesting. Communication with a small child is usually with fewer words, of shorter duration, and with vocabulary appropriate for their age.

An empathetic adult conversation, like those mentioned in previous chapters, usually has a little finesse. Working with children is more about creating and modeling understanding than finding the perfect word or phrase. A chat with a 4- year-old in church day care getting ready for camp can go like this.

Natty – Ok, time to get dressed for day camp. What shirt do you want to wear today?
Sam – I don't want to get dressed!
Natty – You sound mad about not wanting to get dressed.
Sam – I am mad. I don't want to go to camp today.
Natty – You don't want to get dressed because then you won't have to go to camp.
Sam (nodding) – I don't want to go to camp. We had to swim, and I don't want to swim.

Natty – Swimming was hard. You don't want to do it today.

Sam – No. The water was cold, and I was cold. I don't want to go to camp today.

Natty – You didn't like swimming because you were cold. I'll tell your Mom about that and we can see what we can do for next week, ok? Today, there isn't swimming at camp. Today is Thursday, and you only swim on Mondays.

Sam – No swimming today?

Natty – Not today. Today, you'll play ball with Jack and Austin.

Sam – Ok, I want to go to camp today.

Natty – Which shirt do you want to wear?

This could have become a test of wills in a heartbeat. Depending on how strong-willed either the caregiver or child might be, a follow-up to "I don't want to go to camp today" might have been, "Well, it's time to go to camp, so let's get dressed." I imagine most mothers could put themselves in that situation, as well. Off to the races we go.

The empathetic conversation above lasted less than 60 seconds. Natty didn't automatically react to her suggestion of getting dressed not being followed. Sam wasn't just being spiteful or rebellious — there was a problem. He's four, right? He doesn't yet know he can be proactive instead of reactive. When he's 10, he might come home and say he was cold in swimming today, and what can be done to make him warmer. At four, he just doesn't want to go to camp.

Without Natty taking the time to respond instead of react to Sam, she wouldn't know there was an issue at camp. She wants to know. She wants Sam to have a good experience there. There may be something to do about the problem that Sam clearly can't do himself, like having a long-sleeved swim shirt, or a bigger towel. She is the problem solver and can't solve a problem she doesn't know exists. It's worth the minute to find out what's happening in Sam's mind instead of plowing ahead to keep on schedule and trying to wrangle an unwilling four- year-old who is now dreading what isn't even going to happen.

Clearly, there is a responsibility on the caregiver's (or parent's) behalf to respond instead of react in terms of communicating with children. You are, after all, the adult. Just like anyone else, a child may not start any conversation with the actual issue but may throw something out there to get it started and hope you will get them through the maze to the center before it's all over.

When my son was about 6, I was outside gardening when he came to me and asked if he could have a quarter (25 cents) of his saved money. I asked for the reason he wanted it. He told me the kid next door told him he would only be his friend if he gave him a quarter. After he said it, he sat back and waited. He knew it was wrong and he knew he wasn't going to do it, but he needed me to work the process with him, so he understood why. After empathy, a well-placed "What do you think about that?" led us to my son's feelings. We spent a fair amount of time on the subject, but I did my best to do it in a way not to trash the kid who was still going to live 100 feet from our front door, but on whom I was clearly going to have to keep a closer eye.

More recently, when my daughter read the first version of this book, she mentioned with a little intensity that I was not at all empathetic about her wanting to rent out her condo and move downtown for a while. Thinking back, she was right. I wasn't empathetic because I disagreed. Nice, right? Back to Chapter 7 for Mom.

I'm not saying this stuff is easy. I will say it's always worth it. Keep trying for empathy, no matter how hard, whether in a parental or other role. FYI - I still don't want her to move downtown but am much more empathetic talking about it.

Patience as an adult working with children comes and goes, depending on the day and circumstance. The best of parents, staff, and volunteers run out of it occasionally and if you know you are short on it, I would encourage doing the work to build up your storage.   Consistently shutting down a small child who has something to say sets up that child and their older version to either learn their words are not important, or to share those words with someone else.   The older they get, the more you want them to come to you to discuss the important things in their lives. It doesn't just happen.   You earn it by listening to them when they want to talk about small stuff.

All the same concepts and structures apply. Don't forget your RTWYH. Empathize.   Suspend judgment.   Don't interrupt. Please keep in mind any discussion with a child, no matter what age, is an opportunity for you to prove you can be trusted to listen, respect their opinions, and work to understand their perspective. They don't want to hear what you did in the same situation when you were a kid (unless they specifically ask), and probably still don't want advice.

In your role at the church, it can be hard to give one child or student your undivided attention. This is where it's important to know the difference between L1 and L2 conversations. If you think your charge is attempting to involve you in an L2 conversation, can you make it happen without endangering the rest of your kids? Clearly, you can't leave the rest unattended to see to one, but is there the opportunity to allow this conversation to take place? It could, in fact, be important. Research also shows if you do your communication with any child at their eye level (with you stooping or kneeling), they feel more understood.

In the toddler room, this conversation could certainly ha.

Brendan (after following his Sunday School teacher around when she was cleaning up between activities) – Hi, Miss Cissy.

Cissy – Hi, Brendan. Did you like making a picture for your mom?

Brendan – I did, but you are going to be mad at me.

Cissy, squatting down to Brendan's level – You think I'll be mad at you about something.

Brendan – Yes. I didn't do a good job.

Cissy – You think I will be mad because you didn't do a good job on your picture.

Brendan – No, I like my picture.

Cissy – You think I will be mad at you about something else.

Brendan – You will be mad at me.

Cissy – Brendan, what would I be mad about?

Brendan – I had an accident in my pants.

Cissy – Brendan, I'm not mad, and we can get it cleaned up right now. How does that sound?

Brendan – Good. I'm glad you're not mad.

Cissy – I'm glad you told me what happened.

The old saying about "the bigger the kid, the bigger the problem" is no joke. As the world gets more complicated, the questions get bigger and a mess in a little one's pants is a very easily fixed issue as opposed to a decision by a teen that could change their life forever. As someone who works with kids, you have to be ready for both.

In the high school ministry, it could sound more like this.

Josh – I can't come to group on Saturday. I'm grounded.

Doug - – You sound mad.

Josh – I am. My parents are just crazy. They hate me.

Doug – Sounds serious.

Josh – Are you kidding? It's horrible. I don't know if I can take it anymore.

Doug – It seems like it's getting worse for you.

Josh – All the time. The rules are ridiculous, and when I tell them that, they get mad. When I won't follow them because they're ridiculous, I get grounded.

Doug –The rules are the problem. You don't agree with them, and when you say it, you get in trouble.

Josh – Yeah. I don't know if I can stick this out until I leave for college.

Doug – Which is 2 years away.

Josh – It's forever away. Too long.

Doug – I'm wondering what steps you've taken to talk to them about this. You said you've discussed it.

Josh – I don't know if yelling counts as discussion. When I get in trouble, we all get mad and yell, and I tell them how the rules are just not reality. I'm 16! I shouldn't have to be in by 10:30 on the weekends.

Doug – Your choice has been to toss the rules and stay out later.

Josh – Yeah.

Doug, smiling – How's it working for you?

Josh laughs – Not great.

Doug – Ditching the rules gets you grounded, which seems like the opposite of what you want – not going out at all as opposed to being able to stay out later.

Josh – Exactly. It just makes us all madder.

Doug – Any action you can think of to get a better result?

Josh – It doesn't work to talk when everybody is mad.

Doug – You're clear on what doesn't work.

Josh – I could try and talk to them when everybody's calm. I don't know they will change their mind, though.

Doug – But, you think it will be worth a try.

Josh – Yeah. How much worse can it be?

Doug – Anything is better than this.

Josh – What if it doesn't work?

Doug – We can talk again. Maybe you will have more ideas.

Josh – Ok, thanks. I'll text you after.

Doug – How about we pray about it now, before you go?

Josh – Sounds good.

Doug did a good job. He didn't defend the parents, didn't tell Josh he was right, didn't give advice, and did make himself (and

God!) available for Josh now and in the future. The truth is, Doug doesn't know what's best for Josh to do. Josh knows his parents, knows the culture of his home, and probably has the best idea of what steps might be useful. If this escalates, more can be done. There is counseling, a talk with the head of the ministry, a meeting with the parents – there are lots of options.

This, as always, goes back to the boundaries around one's role in the ministry. I have a lot of stories, unfortunately, where a youth pastor or volunteer has made a difficult situation worse by not knowing how to respond to a student's concerns. When there hasn't been training, what's left is a student leader using their own situation as an example and giving a lot of advice. Neither is usually helpful and can be quite harmful.

This harm can be avoided. Train your staff, your volunteers, and yourself, no matter what your position. What's more win-win than a student knowing they can come to you and knowing you're not going to tell them what to do? Don't kids feel like they get enough of that everywhere else?

Train the staff and volunteers well. The next generation (and those after) will be grateful.

14 – Time To Talk

There comes a time when a story is told, and you feel you have a good understanding of what is being said or being asked of you. You have provided empathy, used the discernment available to you, and are now ready to respond. You have much more intelligent information than if you had reacted with solutions or suggestions after the speaker's initial sentences, and as a fabulous byproduct of your patience, so does the speaker. Because of your care, more has been verbalized; the speaker has delved further into the issue than if you had reacted instead of responded. Good job, you.

One of the many bonuses of using empathy correctly is it gives the speaker time and room to better explore their own situation. In a conversation where you are employing all the now-memorized acronyms (RTWYH, ACT, and POE), the person talking can let more of what they are thinking and feeling bubble to the top of their consciousness and come out as words. Being allowed time to speak lets important or hidden parts of a situation into the light. The first two sentences are never the whole deal.

You can now respond from a platform of knowledge, of both the situation and the person. You know more. Your responses are better informed.

To move from listening empathetically to responding can come very naturally, or it might take a transitional sentence or two. There are a couple of choices on how to make the transition.

One way would be by directly providing a summary. You put together the salient parts of the previous discussion in a form and present it to the speaker for their inspection.

Steve – If I understand correctly, you are saying for your new ideas about the church being a more welcoming place to benefit the people coming here, all the employees will need more training. It won't be enough to just train the ushers and welcoming team — the pastoral and administrative staff need to be trained as well.

Karyn – That's right. This is not something just the volunteers can do. It begins when a phone is answered or when a new person passes a staff member in the hallway.

Again, notice there is no judgment or decision-making in the summary. It is all from the speaker's perspective. If your summary is correct, the speaker will agree, and you can go on to responding to one or many of the different facets of the summary.

Steve – I think what you're saying makes a lot of sense. It would be hard for staff to understand these changes without receiving the same training. Where we will find the budget for the training and the time is a different discussion, but you have convinced me about the necessity of it happening. I am impressed with the work you have put into this. Now we need to begin the process about finding the time and budget to make it happen.

This can lead to a solution-focused, but still caring conversation about what steps to take and how to manage any action taken.

Another way to make the transition is to ask if you can now respond. You will listen to people who don't want to stop talking, either with the thought that the more words they say the more likely you will agree, or because they don't believe you understand their viewpoint. If you think you do understand and have summarized the best you can, a request to have the floor is a good next step.

Steve – I believe I understand what you're saying. May I respond?

A more casual rendition of this would be:

Steve – Ok, I think I get it. I haven't missed anything, right? I'd like to respond to a few things.

Using these skills develops a culture of respect, no matter where you are — church, home, work, or the hardware store. Who doesn't like that? They can engender space for creative thought and a new way of dealing with conflict resolution. Used well and often, they create deep understanding.

Isn't it what we all want? To feel valued when we speak, and have the listener show interest and care during the process? As individuals, we spend a fair amount of our lives crafting our identities. We want to be known for who we are, not just for assumptions made about us. As the church, we want to model Christ, to open our doors and hearts in a way that communicates care at the highest degree. It is not too crazy a thought to say using what you're learning will change any culture where you choose to use it. Is there a place you have in your life where creating respect and understanding are not appropriate skills to use?

I think not.

Here's the rub. You are reading the book. I give workshops on this material, and you may have been to one. You have a key, an ace in your pocket. You may, as you use these skills, crave the same skilled treatment for yourself you are providing for others.

I just finished my first quilt. I learned to do it as I went along, thanks to online tutorials. I made a few little mistakes along the way, and then one bigger mistake. It's far from perfect, but it is still a quilt. It's not the best quilt I'll ever make, because I'm going to try and get better, but it will keep the baby warm, it's pink and pretty, and I'll know next time what I did wrong this time. The person receiving it will like it because I worked at it, and she will also like me trying again to do better. It will not be my best quilt, but it's still a quilt, for all that.

Your first attempts at using empathy, being accessible, and having good posture when you speak with someone will not be perfect. These are skills, and like any other, get better with practice. So, practice. Get better. Get great.

This is also something you can model and teach. When you see how this kind of communication can improve all church relationships and outcomes, you may (I wanted to say, "You will," but didn't want to seem pushy) want to share it with those with whom you communicate most often, whether at work or home. Modeling is a great place to start, but like watching a magician, you don't always learn something by watching someone else do it. Training is often necessary.

Share the wealth. Train others, or of you don't feel competent to do it, I'll come and do it for you. (Look in the last chapter for how to find me.) As you provide Care Talk, explain what you're doing so it doesn't seem out of reach to the person benefitting from it; it's a skill they need to develop, just like you did. Make your church and your life empathy-friendly.

This is to be more like Jesus, which will improve your care of those with whom you interact in a church setting and will also directly benefit you. How is that for a great deal?

If you create a culture, anywhere, where empathy is the standard, it becomes a learning community where there are different levels of proficiency, but everyone is working toward the same goal. Part of it means you receive the same respect and care you are providing. In this culture, people are taught to listen well, to respond instead of react, and to understand even if they can't agree. It communicates care and it radiates love.

Where does love come from, again? Oh, right – God. I remember now. "Dear friends, let us continue to love one another, for love comes from God. Anyone who loves is a child of God, and knows God. But anyone who does not love does not know God, for God is love. This is real love – not that we loved God, but that he loved us and sent his Son as a sacrifice to take away our sins. Dear friends, since God loved us that much, we surely ought to love each other." I John 4:7-11. We are called to love. These skills provide practical love in any situation. I could keep talking about it, but that's really the point.

Yesterday at my second home (Joann Fabrics), I picked out six new half-yard pieces of different pink calicos to make another quilt. This one will be better, but I am still proud of my first quilt, for all its mistakes. The first attempt at anything is often a bit messy. It doesn't mean you don't try again.

15 – The Test

I told you there would be a test. I bet you thought I was kidding.

Consider it a way to hammer down the main points, to know what you know and what you don't. I might suggest trying it closed-book first, and for the questions you can't answer, consider it open-book. I bet you know more than you think you do. Get some paper out and we will see.

1. What will you never say to anyone again?
2. What is the difference between reacting and responding?
3. What does RTWYH mean?
4. What is the difference between a Level 1 and a Level 2 conversation?
5. What can go wrong with banter?
6. What is the first tenet of talking with anyone?
7. What is the magic word?
8. What is the difference between empathy and sympathy?
9. Explain "the spotlight."
10. What does ACT stand for?
11. What does POE stand for?
12. What is the empathy equation?
13. What do questions do in any conversation?
14. How many questions can you ask in a row?
15. What word should never begin a sentence?
16. What would you not do when someone is crying?
17. When is self-disclosure appropriate?
18. What are the 3 R's?
19. What is the definition of discernment?

20. What changes in these concepts when speaking with children?
21. What is one way to get the floor when someone is done speaking?

I'm not going to give you the answers, but I will tell you where to find them if you're having trouble.

1. Page 4
2. Page 7
3. Page 16
4. Page 19
5. Page 20
6. Page 24
7. Page 25
8. Page 25
9. Page 30
10. Page 32
11. Page 34
12. Page 39
13. Page 48
14. Page 50
15. Page 50
16. Page 55
17. Page 59
18. Page 63
19. Page 67
20. Page 76
21. Page 83

Now, a couple of questions for extra credit.

22. Which concept in the book do you think will be the easiest to use? For what reasons?

23. Which will be the hardest? For what reasons?
24. How much better can your relationships be as a result of using these skills?

To be intentional at integrating Care Talk into your life, it is important to be able to answer these questions. Lucky for you, you have this trusty reference manual to help. I might suggest reading it again, just for fun.

16 – At the End of the Day

In any conversation, especially with someone coming to the church hurting or trying to be understood, there is a built-in responsibility to do your best.

The questions on the test outline the headliner and sub-head concepts in the book. This isn't complicated. It may not feel natural when you begin, but like any other skill, the more you do it, the better it feels. Eating spaghetti wasn't pretty the first time you tried it, either.

There is tremendous satisfaction when Care Talk is used in everyday circumstances. When you see the look on a speaker's face saying, "Wow, you really do understand!" or when a difficult conversation is made easier or more productive because you listened and empathized instead of pushing your point to the cliff, it will become very clear what the fuss is about.

Everyone has things important enough to master. We all work hard at what means the most to us. I hope I have convinced you how important it is to communicate in a way conveying understanding and care in the church. Work hard at this. It is the usable tool against creating misunderstanding or harm in a place where people come to experience the love of God through imperfect people.

In the church, where the need to learn and worship sits alongside providing love and care, an empathetic culture is imperative. Without it, we will never get to the place of giving as Christ did – beginning with love, listening with intent, and suspending judgment.

Along with the skills you are putting in place, I hope another takeaway has been to treat with respect the words and thoughts of the people with whom you speak, whether you agree or not. This is a person you are facing, not just an idea or concept. These are their thoughts, their soul. Be kind. Be generous in your empathy — it costs you so little. After what Christ has done for us, we can afford it.

Responding to what you hear, not what you think about what you hear is the difference between being able to listen intently and respond from an objective stance or reacting to the words themselves and how they affect you. As hard as it is to contemplate, we are not at the center of everything. Some things said don't have anything to do with us, and the ability to take a step back and respond to someone else without it going through our own filtering process is, when you think about it, common sense.

When you think about the effect of the myriad of conversations happening in and around a church, it's staggering. If staff and volunteers are there to serve God and others, there is absolutely no risk to mastering these skills and using them as indiscriminately as confetti at the end of the Super Bowl. There can be a lot to do once understanding is reached, but you have to get there first. Then, there are steps to be taken. Decisions on how best to serve can be made. There can be healing. Life change. Love can abound.

How fabulous to have accuracy and clarity with which to make these decisions. What the Care Talk skills do is help take away assumption. They take away the fog we can easily create when we layer our own thoughts, judgments, and inner dialogue on someone else's words.

Time to see for yourself. I'd love to hear about your successes and attempts, so feel free to contact me at caretalkshannon@gmail.com if you'd care to share them. Please know I am rooting for you, and I completely believe in this process. Know it is tried and true, and not the new fad.

I do workshops, so if you want me to come and teach you, let me know.

Most importantly, don't give up. Ever. Try and try again. Then again. Ok, one more time. The result will be the church, God's almighty church, the hands and heart of God on Earth with which we have been entrusted, will dramatically improve.

May your efforts be blessed.

Acknowledgments

This began as a whisper from God in response to my holy discontent. It came to life with assistance.

I so thank Tim Auch for his strategic process and never-ending help with this project from idea to birth. Your belief in the concepts and substantial generosity with time, skill, and creativity are forever appreciated.

As always, I thank my husband, Lee Plate, for his ever-consistent support for my ideas and schemes, and his willingness to go anywhere and do anything to make them happen.